REMODELING
LIVING SPACE

SMITHMARK

© 1993 Dragon's World Ltd

Photographs by Jon Bouchier, Simon Butcher, Simon Wheeler.

Illustrations by Kuo Kang Chen, Steve Cross, Paul Emra, Pavel Kostal, Janos Marffy, Sebastian Quigley, Laurie Taylor, Brian Watson, Andrew Green.

This edition published in 1993 by SMITHMARK Publishers Inc., 16 East 32nd Street, New York, NY 10016.

SMITHMARK books are available for bulk purchase for sales promotion and premium use. For details write or call the manager of special sales, SMITHMARK Publishers Inc., 16 East 32nd Street, New York, NY 10016; (212) 532-6600.

Produced by Dragon's World Ltd, 26 Warwick Way, London SW1V 1RX, England.

Editor: Dorothea Hall
Designers: Bob Burroughs, Mel Raymond
Art Director: Dave Allen
Editorial Director: Pippa Rubinstein

ISBN 0-8317-4629-9

Printed in Italy

10 9 8 7 6 5 4 3 2 1

NOTICE
The authors, consultants and publishers have made every effort to make sure the information given in this book is reliable and accurate. They cannot accept liability for any damage, mishap or injury arising from the use or misuse of the information.

CONTENTS

INTRODUCTION

If your family is fast becoming cramped for space,
and moving to a bigger house is not feasible, then you will be
researching the different ways in which you can create the
additional living space in your home that will most satisfactorily
encompass your needs.
The following pages offer a wide variety of options — from
simple room dividers to full attic conversions and built-on room
extensions — with all the practical know-how required for the
non-professional homebuilder to achieve excellent results every
time. Special information is also given for finishing and
carrying out any repairs to the surrounding areas that are
affected by re-building.

INTRODUCTION

When space becomes cramped at home, it is not always necessary to move to a larger house to solve the problem. Often, more usable space can be arranged using the resources already at your disposal – and usually at a much lower cost and less frustrating than that of moving.

There are several ways in which you can gain a substantial amount of extra living space in your home – from simply partitioning off larger rooms to making two or more smaller rooms, opening up under-stair areas, or removing a wall to enlarge a room to converting attic space and building a single-storey, ground floor extension.

Room divisions, and very often attic conversions, can be carried out without the need for filing with your local building department, but a permit may be required to build a separate extension. As local laws can vary considerably in different locations, it is always best to check first with your local building code (see page 9).

Remodeling

The size of a room, its shape, and the number of rooms you have can each present particular problems – a growing family may mean you could do with more bedrooms, or an additional bathroom to ease that early morning traffic jam, perhaps even separate dens for the older and younger elements of the family. Many people have also to look after elderly or infirm relatives, in which case an extra powder room or bathroom and bedroom can be very useful if not a full-scale extension.

Extra rooms can be provided by partitioning off larger ones with wood-framed walls complete with access doors. In the same way, large open-plan rooms can be divided into smaller, cosier rooms if that is what you prefer. In the latter case, a partial or half-height partition would provide an effective division between, say, the dining and living areas of a room while retaining the spacious, airy feel of an open-plan layout.

Dealing with doors

Access routes between rooms are important, if you are to get the best from your home. Very often doors are not placed in the most convenient locations, there is no reason why you should not reposition doors, or make new doorways between adjoining rooms where none existed before; or block off redundant doorways where say, two rooms have been joined into one.

Using similar skills, you can improve the light of gloomy rooms by installing larger windows and, perhaps, even more than one.

Converting an attic

Converting an attic to provide extra living space may be the answer to solving the needs of a growing family and their interests. It will obviously involve more expense than a simple room division, (particularly if you need to install a window and staircase) but it is worth remembering that such a conversion will add greatly to the overall value of your house.

Handling the paperwork

All the work done to convert the attic into living space must comply with the requirements of the Zoning and Building Codes, and before work can begin plans must be drawn up and submitted to your local Building Department for approval. They will be able to advise you on any aspects of the work about which you are unsure, and will probably want to make several checks on the work as it progresses.

The Codes vary so greatly across the country that what may need approval on in one area does not need approval in another. If you feel unsure, check with your local Building Department or consult with a local professional Architect or Engineer before starting.

There are two routes you can take to getting professional help: you can either employ an architect to design the conversion and then get him to supervise the builder who does the work, or approach a specialist remodeler, who will both design the conversion and carry out the work. In the first instance you will get something that suits your needs exactly, whereas in the latter you may get a variation on one of several standard plans. However, there may be quite a difference in price, so do get quotes from different companies for comparison.

In many cases the architect or contractor will handle the Building Code side of the job for you, perhaps relieving you of a considerable headache. Both will also be able to tell you if the structure of the roof makes a conversion possible at all. Sometimes it is possible to remove major supporting members which are in the way and support the load they carried by making one of the internal partitions load-bearing or by inserting strong wooden beams in the framework of the walls or floor. In other areas, essential supporting framing may be left in place and the internal partitions built off them — in some instances the resulting shapes being adapted for bookshelves or storage space, for example.

Extensions

If you need more rooms and there is simply no other way you can get more room from the existing layout, the answer may be to build on an extra room or rooms at the side or rear of the house.

Code requirements

As with an attic conversion (see page 64), you will need a building permit for an extension, but it is as well to check with the local Building Department. In some areas the Building Code requires that any addition is built in the same style and in matching materials as the main part of the house. In this situation, even if the extension is within the permitted size and does not project above the roof line or beyond the front of the building, you would still need a building permit.

Regardless of the Zoning situation, all the work must comply with the Building Code, so early contact with your local Building Inspector is essential. He will want to see plans of the extension, being particularly interested in the foundations and will advise you on the requirements for your specific situation. He will also want to inspect the work as it progresses.

With a purpose built extension you should employ an architect to design it and take care of the Building Code matters. He will also supervise the building work. This should be done by a competent builder, but you may be able to reduce the cost if he will agree to you doing the less critical parts of the job.

A standard contract should be taken out with the builder that defines his responsibilities, specifies costs, starting and completion dates and gives details of how payment will be made.

Prefabricated extensions are often designed for assembly by the purchaser, although the manufacturer can send his own erection team to do it for you; he may even insist on this if the extension is above a certain size.

Obviously, any extension will be costly and you should give considerable thought as to how you will pay for it. In some cases you may qualify for a guaranteed loan through the federal government. You may be able to extend your mortgage, or get a loan from a bank or finance company. It is worth shopping around to get the best terms.

Skills and techniques

The methods for carrying out all of these alterations are covered on the following pages, together with ways of correcting defects in the fabric of the house so that whether you are just moving in or have lived in your house for many years, you can remodel your living space to the very highest standards. And you will not only be improving home comforts but adding to the overall value of the house.

Additional restrictions

In addition to the Building Code your house may be part of a residential community or association which also places restrictions or limitations on the type of alterations that may be made to the property. Generally this extends only to the type and style of fences or a ban on blacktop drive ways, but in some areas – a neighborhood of Victorian gingerbread houses for example – it may restrict the architectural style of any new work. Further restrictions to the type of alteration you may make to your home may be made by the mortgage holder or by the house insurer. Always check with your insurance agent to make sure that your home owners policy is not invalidated by the construction work. Some insurers will insist that at least part of the work – usually the electrics or plumbing and heating – is carried out by professionals.

Houses built before the Building Code took effect are not required to comply to the Code unless they are altered.

Building permits

A building permit will probably be required if you plan to do the following:

1 Alter or change the external appearance of your house. For example if you: add a porch; add a screen in a porch; add or remove a window or door, or if you build a fence or wall.
2 Do any electrical work.
3 Do any plumbing work.
4 Add or remove any structural element.
5 Build an addition to your house.
6 Erect a separate building on your property.

Applying for a building permit

To obtain a building permit, a set of plans showing your proposed alterations must be submitted to the local Building Department where they will be checked for compliance with the National and local Building Code. If the plans are up to code a permit will be issued, usually for a small fee. The permit will be valid for one year after which time a new application must be made if the work has not started. The permit must be displayed prominently at the job site for inspection by any interested authority.

THE BUILDING CODE

Whatever you plan to alter or build in your home it is likely that you will need to apply for a building permit before commencing the work. All remodeling, renovation and new construction work in your area is bound to certain rules and regulations known as the Building Code. The purpose of the Building Code is to provide minimum standards of construction and to make sure that your home is safe for occupancy.

All communities have adopted the Federal Building Code as a minimum standard, and to this has probably been added any additional State Building Codes which apply to the community. Finally the town or village may have adopted its own regulations which take into account local building standards, local building practices, materials or preferences in addition to the minimum standards set down by the National Building Code. This entire body of regulation makes up your local Building Code, so before starting any work in your home make sure you pick up a current copy of the Code from your local Building Department at the town hall. At this time you may be able to discuss your improvement plans with the Building Inspector himself or an assistant.

Zoning

You will find that all property in your community is divided into lots. Each lot has a number and a record of all the lots is kept at the town hall. The lots are further grouped into zones set aside for specific purposes which have been determined by the local community. The zones may be designated as either residential, commercial or manufacturing. Residential zones will probably be broken down into several different types such as zone A, zone AA and zone B or maybe zone R1, zone R2, zone R3 and so on. It is important to determine in which zone your property lies as each zone may have separate requirements under the local Code. Depending in which zone your property is located, the Code will cover such items as minimum lot size; front side and rear yard setbacks; height restrictions; positioning of wells and sewage systems; accessory buildings and occupancy requirements.

At various stages of the construction work you may be required to call in the local building inspector to check the work for compliance, for instance, before and after any footings have been made. This checking procedure ensures that the work is indeed being carried out according to the approved plans and that the method of construction and the quality of the materials is up to the standard set out in the Building Code. Although this procedure may not be necessary on your particular job, however, the Building Inspector may call by at any time to check on the progress of the work.

Always be sure to complete the job according to the approved plans. If you are in any doubt, call the building inspector and ask his advice, never try to guess. This could be a waste of your time and money as any work not covered by the approved plans or not up to the standards of the code may be condemned at any stage of the building.

Seeking a variance

If your plans are rejected by the building department for non-compliance you will receive a notification of the reasons given. In some cases this may be simply dealt with by getting your building contractor to amend the plans making sure all the changes are incorporated before re-submitting them.

In other cases the layout of your property may make it impossible to comply with the requirements of the code. In this case you may seek an exception to the law by filing an application with the Zoning Board of Review. When filing for an exemption, evidence supporting your position must be presented with your application, together with a block plan showing all lots within a specified distance including all buildings and marked with owners' names and addresses. A plan of your lot showing the existing structures, and plans and elevations of the proposed work must also be submitted. A decision will be made after a public meeting of the Board during which any member of the public may speak for or against the project.

CHAPTER 1

WORKING ON THE INTERIOR

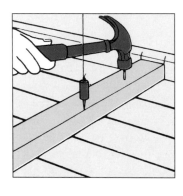

You may simply wish to enlarge a window to get a better view of your backyard or remove a wall to enlarge a room — but in looking for ways to remodel your living space, all areas within the house offer scope for consideration.

This chapter illustrates, for example, many types of room dividers and partitions which are some of the simplest and most effective forms of breaking up larger rooms to give cosier living spaces; as well as decorative archways, doorways and service hatches — all excellent means of bridging the enlarged room which will greatly improve accessibility with style and economy.

DIVIDING THE SPACE

Partitions can be used in most homes to make best use of available space, turning large or awkwardly-shaped rooms into more manageable accommodation.

The large, L-shaped room is common to many homes, yet it is not the most convenient of shapes to furnish or heat. By building a partition with an access door across one of the legs of the 'L' you can produce two smaller, rectangular rooms which are much cosier and more easily heated.

Long, narrow rooms also produce their own particular problems, such as giving the impression of being like tunnels or causing difficulties in positioning furniture. The tendency is to put everything around the walls, leaving a large bare area in the center of the room. By building a partition that spans, say, only half of the room's width, you can create two distinct areas (for living and dining perhaps) without completely losing the feeling of being in one large room. Furniture can then be grouped more effectively into sitting arrangements and dining areas. You can achieve the same effect by building a waist-high partition across the room, but in this case there would be much more of an open-plan feel to the room. Such a partition would also provide some useful shelf space along the top, or for a tier of shelves above.

Obviously, if you are using a partition to make two rooms out of one, you will have to arrange access to the new room. The easiest way is to build a door in the partition. However, this means that you must walk through one room to reach the other and that might not always be convenient, especially if the rooms are used as bedrooms. To overcome this problem you can either make a new doorway through one of the original walls of the room or build a second partition at right angles to the first to form a small lobby, from which both rooms can be entered separately and maintain a sense of privacy.

Providing daylight

An important point to consider when partitioning a room is the availability of daylight in both new rooms. You may find that the only suitable position for the partition means that one room has no window at all. In this situation, you can provide a fair degree of natural light by incorporating panes of glass (clear or frosted depending on the purpose of the room) along the top of the partition. You could even include a glass door.

Creating storage space

Partitions can be very useful for creating storage. By building what is effectively a false wall across the end of a room, you can use the space between it and the original wall for inset shelving, cabinets and even walk-in closets. This can be very handy if there is a small room next to a large one, since by cutting an opening in the original dividing wall and arranging the internal divisions of the storage space carefully, you will provide a storage facility for both rooms.

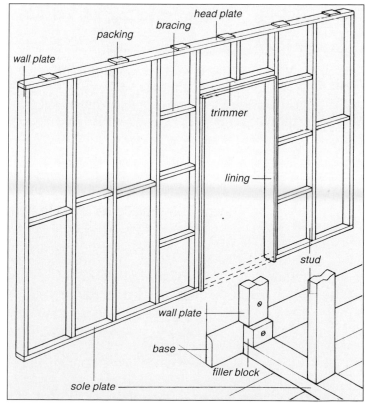

Except for the wall plates and bracing, you should build a stud framework flat on the floor; lift and wedge it into position, fit the bracing and wall plates and cut out the threshold of the door. Fit a block baseboard (inset) so that the drywall edge is fully supported.

A bathroom formed by partitioning off part of a larger room. The confined space is visually enlarged by the overall tiling of the walls and bath platform, and light is admitted through a glass block wall.

BUILDING A STUD PARTITION

The easiest form of partition to build is the wood frame variety – it is ideal for dividing one bedroom into two, making an extra powder room or bathroom, or splitting a dining area from a kitchen or living room. The wood frame is simply nailed together and faced with drywall on each side; it is easily adapted for doorways, pass throughs or windows. Being essentially hollow, it can also be used to conceal electrical wiring and water pipes.

The framework comprises a number of uprights called "studs" fitted between lengths of wood spanning the width of the ceiling and floor. These are called the "head plate" and "sole plate" respectively. Short horizontal lengths of wood are fixed between the uprights to brace them and support the cladding. In most cases 2 × 3in rough sawn softwood is ideal for the studs and bracing, with 1½ × 3in for the head and sole plates. If the partition is to carry a lot of weight such as shelves or cupboards, a larger size should be used, say 2 × 4in.

Planning the partition

Deciding where to put the partition is the first thing to do so that you end up with two usable rooms. If possible arrange things so that each new room gets the benefit of a window, but do not be tempted to set the partition so that it divides a window in two. Not only does this look dreadful, but in some cases it is also illegal. If you cannot provide a window for each room, glaze the upper portion of the partition so that you can "borrow" some natural light from the room with the window. Similarly, if you cannot provide an opening window for each new room, you will be required to install a form of mechanical ventilation.

Important considerations are the layouts of floor and ceiling joists since the head and sole plates will be attached to these. Ideally, the partition should run at right angles to the joists so that its weight is spread across them. If this is not possible, it must be directly above a joist. With a solid floor, there is no problem.

If the head plate does not span the ceiling joists and does not come below a single joist because the ceiling joists do not line up with the floor joists, you should nail lengths of 2in sq blocking between the ceiling joists and attach the head plate to these.

Before you begin work, check under the floor and above the ceiling for any cables or pipes that might be damaged by nails or screws. It is also a good idea to check with your local Building Code before carrying out any structural work.

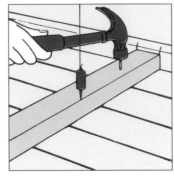

1 Nailing the sole plate to the floor joists; mark the line of the wall on the ceiling and hang a plumb-line to give the position on the floor.

2 Screwing the head plate to the ceiling joists through countersunk clearance holes; prop the wood in position with one of the studs.

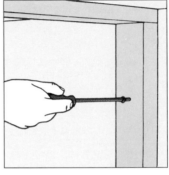

3 Fixing one end of the stud to the wall with screws and wall-plugs, after tapping it into position; repeat for the other end stud.

4 Marking the position of a stud on the sole plate, using an offcut; the studs are usually spaced at 16in centers.

5 After setting the foot of the stud on the squared marks, tapping into the vertical position; check that the foot is still on the marks.

6 Toe-nailing the stud using an offcut for support; drive in two more nails on the other side and repeat at the top of the stud.

Erecting the framework

Begin by cutting the head and sole plates to length; whenever possible buy wood long enough so that you can span the room with one piece. Nail the sole plate to the joists through the floorboards using 4in long common nails or fix it to a concrete floor with 4in long No. 10 woodscrews and wall plugs or with masonry

1 Toe-nailing in-line bracing; the block below, temporarily nailed to the stud, provides support during nailing.

2 Nailing into the ends of staggered bracing; this method of construction is stronger and easier to erect.

3 Fixing an extra stud over a door-opening; the bracing here is the lintel for the doorway and must be set into the stud at each side.

4 Screwing the lining to the stud; the side linings are rebated into the head lining and should be flush with the gypsumboard.

BRACING THE STUDS

With all the studs in place, now fit the bracing. If you intend cladding the partition with standard 8ft sheets of gypsumboard, place the bracing in a row 4ft from the floor. If the partition is taller than 8ft, a second row of bracing should be fitted to support the upper edges of the drywall panels and the lower edges of the panels above them.

For strength, stagger the bracing above and below each other – this makes fitting easier, too – but if they are to support the edges of two sheets of drywall they must all be in line. In this case, the center line of each brace must coincide with the edges of the panels. Mark the brace positions on the studs with a pencil and level to make sure they are all horizontal.

Cut the bracing so that it is a close fit between the studs but not over-length, otherwise it will push the studs out of true.

Begin fitting the bracing at the wall end of the partition and work in towards the center. A block of wood nailed to the wall stud will support the end of the first brace while you nail through the second stud into the other end of the brace. Use two nails. Then toe-nail the inner end of the brace to the wall stud. If the bracing is to be lined up, repeat this procedure for each one; if it is to be staggered, simply drive nails through the studs into the ends of the brace.

The ends of the bracing ("header") over a doorway must be fitted in 1½in deep slots cut in the sides of the adjacent studs. Cut down the side of each slot with a back saw and remove the waste with a 1in bevel-edged chisel, working in from each end, or use a double stud at the header ends to support it.

Trimming the doorway
Having completed the framework, you can remove the section of sole plate from the threshold of the doorway. Simply saw through each end level with the studs on each side. Then clad the framework with gypsumboard (see page 14), trimming the panels round the doorway flush with the studs and header.

The door opening should be trimmed with lengths of 4 × 1in planed softwood that fit flush with the faces of the gypsumboard panels on each side. Cut a length to fit snugly between the studs at the top and screw this to the header. Then screw two longer pieces to the studs on each side of the door opening.

Finally, cut pieces of molding to fit round the door opening, mitering their corners at 45°. Nail the molding to the edges of the trimming pieces with 1in finishing nails, driving their heads below the surface.

anchors or masonry nails. Screw the head plate to the ceiling joists.

Cut the studs for each end of the partition, leaving them a fraction over-length so that they will be a tight fit between the head and sole plates, and screw them to the wall. Use 4in long No.10 screw and wall plugs.

Then mark off the positions of the other studs along the sole plate, making sure their centers are 16in or no more than 24in apart. They should be positioned so that the edges of the cladding material will meet along their center lines (standard sheets of drywall are 4ft wide). If the partition is to have a door in it, the stud positions on each side of the opening must be adjusted to allow for the door width and the thickness of the lining (see page 11).

Measure and cut each stud individually as there is no guarantee that head and sole plates will be parallel.

Set each stud in place, making sure it is vertical with a spirit level, and fix it by driving 3 or 4in common nails at an angle through the side of the stud into the head and sole plate (known as toe-nails).

PLASTER-BOARDING

Plasterboard is a sandwich of gypsum plaster held between two layers of thick paper. You can plaster over it, paint or paper it to match other walls. It is ideal for cladding a timber framed partition, the panels being simply nailed in place.

Always handle plasterboard carefully; it is easily broken. If you intend plastering it, fit the gray side outermost, but if you want to paint or paper over it leave the ivory-coloured side showing.

Fix all the full-size panels to the framework first then the smaller pieces, completing one side at a time. If the partition does not span the room fully, work from the outer end towards the wall.

Cutting

To cut plasterboard, use a sharp knife and steel straightedge; after cutting through one side, stand the board on edge and snap it back to break the plaster. Cut through the remaining paper layer. For right-angle cuts mark both sides of the panel and cut through from both sides. Trim full panels to measure about 1in less than the floor-to-ceiling height; this will allow you to push them up tight against the ceiling with a "footlifter" before nailing.

Fix the board to the frame, using 1¼in galvanized plasterboard nails or screws, spacing them at 6in intervals and working outwards from the center of the panel. Keep the fixings at least 1½in from the edge of the panel to prevent them from breaking the edge. Drive the nails or screws in so that their heads come just below the surface. This is enough to allow for a thin skim of filler.

To fill the joints, apply a layer of proprietary joint filler then press in a length of paper or fiberglass jointing tape. Apply more filler up to the level of the surrounding plasterboard, feathering the edges with a damp sponge. When dry, apply one or two thin layers of joint finish, again feathering the edges.

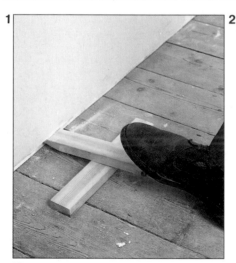

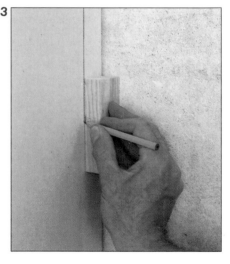

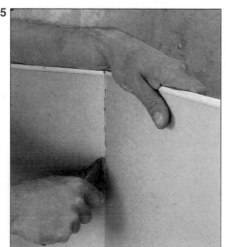

1 Lifting a sheet of drywall with a foot-lifter; the gap at the bottom will be covered by the baseboard.

2 Nailing the drywall to the wooden framework; nail at 6in intervals and at least ½in in from the edges.

3 Scribing against an uneven wall; cut the board to shape with a fine-toothed general-purpose saw.

4 Cutting drywall; score through the paper on one side with a sharp knife and snap the board smartly backwards.

5 Separating the two pieces; bend the board slightly to give a cutting guide and cut through the other paper layer.

CONSTRUCTING A BLOCKWORK WALL

Although a wood-framed partition is easy to build, it does not provide the most effective sound insulation and it will need extra strengthening if it is to carry shelves or cabinets. In situations such as this, a partition built from lightweight concrete blocks is much more suitable. However, you cannot build such a partition on an upper floor, since even a reinforced concrete floor is unlikely to be strong enough to carry the load of a concrete block partition. A concrete first floor makes an ideal foundation and even a suspended wood first floor will do if a full-width wood sole plate is put down first, but check with your local Code.

Before starting work, the floor, walls and ceiling should be stripped of all coverings and any coving and base cut away with a chisel to clear the blocks. The easiest way to mark the position of the partition is with a chalked plumbline, snapping it against the floor to leave two parallel chalk lines the width of the blocks. Continue these lines up the walls and across the ceiling making sure they are vertical.

For strength, it is best to tie the partition to adjacent walls by cutting recesses in them to accept the end blocks of alternate courses or similarly by using galvanized metal ties screwed to the walls and buried in the blockwork mortar joints. Nailing a guide batten to the wall against one of the chalk lines is also a good idea to help with the alignment.

Trowel a 6in wide layer of mortar (1 part masonry cement: 6 parts soft sand) across the floor to span the chalk lines on it, leveling it out to about ⅜in thick. Then scribe a guide line through the mortar in line with the chalk marks on the end walls, using the point of your trowel and a long straight-edged plank. The blocks should be laid up to this line.

1 On a solid floor, spreading a mortar bed on the floor between vertical guide battens.

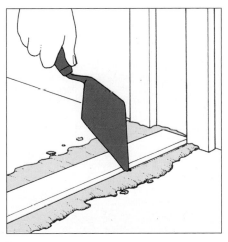
2 Scribing a guide line in the mortar for one face of the wall set squarely against a straight-edge.

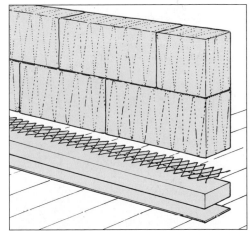
3 On a timber floor, build on a sole plate with a metal lath; underfelt beneath helps to absorb sound.

•CHECKPOINT•

CONCRETE BLOCKS

There are many different types of concrete block to choose from, but the best types for building an internal partition are known as aerated blocks (A). These are light in weight, so they are easy to handle – an important quality since they are twice the size of a normal brick. This fact also means that you can build a full-height partition relatively quickly. You can drill them, knock nails into them or, using a general-purpose saw, cut channels in them (B) to conceal electric cables and pipework. Sound will not pass through them as easily as it would a woodframed partition, nor will heat. Aerated blocks should be laid in the same manner as bricks in a "stretcher" bond pattern with mortar joints. Their normal size is 17 × 8½ × 4in. For finishing, you can either plaster them directly or nail on battens and fix a gypsumboard cladding to the battens.

LAYING THE BLOCKS

Before laying the blocks it is as well to carry out a dummy run on the first two courses, so you will know how best to arrange them to keep the number of cut blocks to a minimum. Set them out along the layer of mortar in line with the scribed mark, spacing them a finger-thickness apart.

If the partition is to have a door in it, now is the time to position the frame. Nail battens across the corners of the frame and across the bottom to hold it square and prop it up with a batten nailed to the top.

Now begin laying the blocks properly. It is best to build up about four courses of blocks at each end of the partition first and then stretch a stringline between them as a guide for the blocks in the middle.

Trowel a layer of mortar onto the original thin layer and "butter" the end of the first block with more mortar. Set the block in place against the scribed line and against the wall to form a neat mortar joint. Tap the block level and upright with the handle of the trowel. Repeat the procedure for the next block in the course and lay two or three more before working back towards the wall with the second, third and fourth courses. Collect the mortar that is squeezed out from between the blocks for reuse.

Make sure the blocks butt up to the guide batten and check them every now and again with a mason's level to ensure that you are keeping the courses upright and level. Tie each alternate course to the wall with galvanized metal wall ties. Similarly secure the door frame to the blockwork; build up the center of the partition.

If you need to cut any blocks, do this with a bricklayer's chisel and hammer. Measure up the block and scribe a cutting line on all four sides with the end of the chisel. Then tap gently along this line with the chisel. Finally, lay the block face up, set the chisel in the center of the cutting line and strike it a sharp blow which will separate the two halves of the block.

1 Dry-laying to check for fit; allow a finger-thickness between blocks for mortar. Vertical battens give support until the mortar hardens.
2 Spreading the mortar bed on the floor; scribe the line of one face of the wall in the mortar with the point of the trowel.
3 "Buttering" one end with mortar before laying the block; place this end against the previous block.
4 Laying the block on the mortar bed, flush with the scribed line.
5 Tamping the block level with the adjacent block· using the trowel handle; check each block as it is laid with a spirit-level.
6 Securing a metal frame-clamp to the side wall; tie alternate courses in this way.
7 Checking the face of the blockwork for alignment; use a long spirit-level or straight-edge and check in a number of directions.
8 Nail temporary "strainer" battens across a door-frame to keep it square and support it in an upright position with a plank nailed to the top.
9 A door-height opening needs a lintel above it to support the blockwork; a course of bricks on top will align with the blockwork.

•CHECKPOINT•

FITTING SERVICES IN A PARTITION WALL

Careful planning is essential when arranging a partition — this extends to working out cable and pipe runs and installing them as you build.

Services in stud partitions
The time to put either cables or pipes into a stud partition is when the framework is finished.

Whenever installing cables or pipes in any kind of wall, remember that they must always run vertically or horizontally directly to or from each fitting.

Electricity
To run cable through the framework of a stud partition, bore a ¾in hole through either the head plate or sole plate into the ceiling or floor void as appropriate and, depending on the direction from which the cable is to come, drill similar holes through the centers of any bracing that cross the cable route.

Feed in the cable, leaving plenty of excess. Cut a hole in the drywall for the fitting and feed the end of the cable through this as you fit the drywall in place.

Plumbing
Working in the same way, make sure the holes you drill through the framework are larger than the diameter of the pipe. This will make manouvering them into place easier and allow them to expand and contract as the temperature fluctuates. Keep the number of joints inside the partition to the bare minimum and make sure you test any plumbing system before you finish the cladding; if there is a leaking joint you will be able to rectify it. If the pipes are to drop down from the ceiling you could remove a floorboard in the room above and feed them down through the partition from there.

Alternatively, pipes can be clipped into notches cut in the edges of the bracing and studs. Using a back saw and bevel-edge chisel, cut notches wide enough to accept a pipe clip of the right size and deep enough so that the pipe does not touch the drywall cladding.

Services in blockwork partitions
Electrical cables can be run across the surface of the blocks in pipes and held in place with clips.

For pipes, use a hammer and bricklayer's chisel to cut out a channel across the face of the blocks, making it wide enough to accept the appropriate size of pipe clip and deep enough so that the pipe will be flush with the surface.

Hot water pipes
Should you want to bury a hot water pipe, it is best to run it through another pipe of the next size up, which will act as a sleeve and allow for expansion.

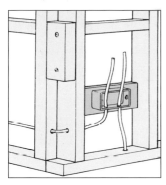

1 Mount and outlet box in a stud wall on a brace nailed between two studs; drill holes for cables, allowing plenty of clearance.

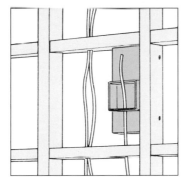

2 Mount switch boxes on boards nailed to the studs; leave plenty of slack in the cables to avoid straining the connections.

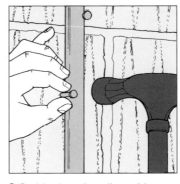

3 On blockwork walls, cable can be run through conduit nailed to the blocks; this will be concealed when the wall is plastered.

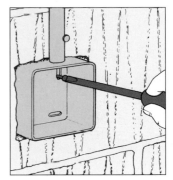

4 An outlet mounting-box is partially recessed into blockwork, and then plugged and screwed in the recess.

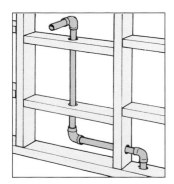

5 Pipework can be fed through holes drilled in the studs and bracing; this will provide adequate support.

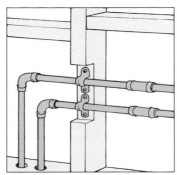

6 Alternatively, cut notches in the framework and secure the pipe with saddle-clips.

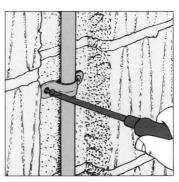

7 Chase cold water pipes in blockwork and secure them with saddle-clips plugged and screwed to the blocks.

8 Hot pipes may be boxed in with wooden battens or chased within an outer pipe to allow for expansion and contraction.

•CHECKPOINT•

PLASTERING TECHNIQUES

Plaster is an excellent and inexpensive material for giving a smooth, hard surface to an internal wall so that it is ready for painting or wallpapering.

There are many types of plaster, but they can be divided into two basic types: gypsum-based and cement-based. The former are used solely for indoor work, whereas the latter are mainly used outdoors for rendering walls. Cement-based plasters do have a use indoors, however, and that is to finish external walls that might be subject to damp penetration; damp will attack a gypsum plaster and cause it to crumble.

Modern plasters come premixed with lightweight fillers such as perlite or vermiculite, which give a higher degree of thermal insulation and fire resistance and should be mixed with clean water.

Plaster is normally applied to the wall in two layers. The first, called a "floating" coat, is intended to even out the irregularities in the wall surface, so it is kept fairly thick – about ⅜in being usual. The second, finishing coat is spread much thinner ⅛in or so – and carefully troweled off to a smooth finish.

Different types of building materials absorb water at different rates and if too much water is absorbed from the fresh plaster, it will dry too quickly and crack.

For example, bricks and lightweight building blocks absorb water quickly and are termed high suction surfaces. On the other hand, materials such as concrete and gypsumboard do not absorb water that quickly and are termed low suction. You must choose a plaster to match the surface; but if in doubt, the best thing to do is coat the entire wall with a bonding agent which will make a low suction surface.

Browning plaster should be used for the floating coat on high suction surfaces and Bonding plaster on low suction surfaces. Finish plaster can be used for the finishing coat in both cases.

Only buy plaster as you need it since it has a limited shelf life. A 22lb bag of Browning or Bonding plaster should cover an area of about 1.8yd² at a depth of ⅜in. The same quantity of Finish plaster, spread thinly, should cover an area about 6yd².

In addition to a couple of clean buckets and a long level, you will need some special plastering tools: a spot board about 3ft square and supported on trestles or an old table to hold the mixed plaster while you work; a hawk for carrying small quantities of plaster to the wall; a rectangular metal plasterer's trowel; a wooden float for producing flat surfaces (with a few nails knocked into the end it can double as a "scratcher" for scoring the floating coat before applying the finishing coat); and a 5ft length of 1 × 3in planed wood for leveling the plaster surface.

MIXING PLASTER

Cleanliness is essential when mixing plaster, since any dirt present in the mix will affect the drying time. Always use clean tap water for mixing and have a separate bucket of water for cleaning the tools as you work.

Mix the plaster and water in equal volumes in a clean bucket, adding the plaster to the water by sprinkling it on top and breaking up any lumps between your fingers. When the water has soaked into all the plaster, use a thick piece of wood to stir the plaster into a smooth consistency, (Finish plaster should resemble runny ice-cream), and make sure there are no lumps.

Wet the spot board and turn out the plaster on to it, kneading it with the trowel. If the mix appears too wet, sprinkle on a little more plaster and mix in with the trowel.

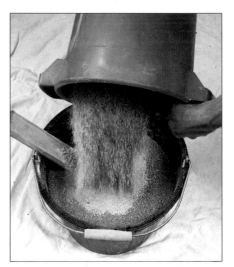

Right: Mixing equal volumes of plaster and water; pouring the plaster onto the water helps to break up any lumps of plaster.

Far left: Plasterer's tools:
A hawk
B bucket
C float
D straightedge
E scratcher
F metal trowel
G spiritlevel
H spotboard.

Left: Kneading the plaster with a trowel after pouring it onto a wet spot-board; add more plaster if it is too runny.

SETTING OUT FOR PLASTERING

One problem the beginner faces when tackling a plastering job is that of producing a floating coat that is uniform in thickness and level over the entire wall. The answer is to divide the wall into sections and use the dividers as depth guides.

Space the dividers as close together or as far apart as you like, but a suitable distance is about 3ft.

Dividing the wall

There are various methods for dividing the wall into bays, and a traditional way is to trowel narrow strips of plaster from floor to ceiling. Known as "screeds", these strips of plaster are allowed to harden, then more plaster is spread on the wall between them and brought up to their level, using a long straightedge placed across the screeds to check.

The problem with the screeding method is being able to get the plaster strips to the right thickness in the first place. Small blocks of wood, known as "dots", can be fixed to the wall at the top and bottom of the screed position and used as thickness guides by setting a straightedge between them.

An easier way is to use wooden "grounds". These are lengths of planed, ⅜in thick by about 2in wide softwood, which are fixed to the wall with masonry nails. Since you plaster only one bay at a time, you need only two grounds per wall and, therefore, you can move them along as you work.

After setting out the first bay, you can apply a floating coat between the two wooden grounds, striking it off level with a long wooden straightedge called a "rule". Then, having let the plaster harden off for a while, you should carefully pull one ground from the wall and nail it back on further along the wall to make a second bay.

Continue applying the floating coat in this way until you have completed the job.

When fitting wooden grounds it is essential that they are set vertically, otherwise the plaster surface will be out of true. Use a long mason's level to check that they are upright and, if necessary, slip small wooden shims as packing pieces behind the grounds to bring them into line.

Using metal lath

An alternative to using wood grounds is the metal screed bead which you can buy from your builder's supply house. It does the same job as the ground but is designed to be left in place on the wall; it disappears under the finishing coat of plaster.

The center of the bead is formed into a raised, inverted U-shape, the depth of which is equal to the depth of the floating coat, and on each side there is expanded metal mesh. You can cut it by snipping through the mesh with metal snips then sawing through the bead with a hacksaw.

Beading is fixed to the wall with "dabs" – blobs of plaster troweled on to the wall. Push the beading into the dabs then check with a level.

Allow the plaster to harden off and then use the beads as thickness guides for the floating coat.

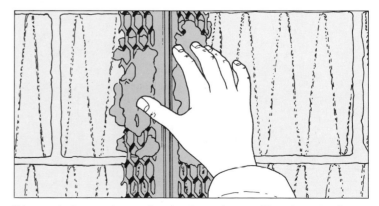

1 Setting up guide battens (grounds) before plastering; pack out any low areas with card or plywood and fix to the blockwork with masonry nails.

2 Checking the level of the front faces of the grounds; use a straight-edge to ensure a uniform distance from the blockwork.

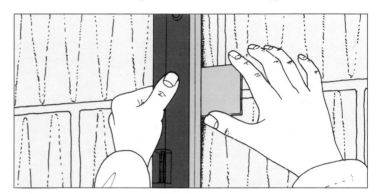

3 Instead of grounds, a galvanized metal screed bead can be fixed to the wall on dabs of plaster; this is left in the plaster.

PLASTERING WALLBOARD

You need only apply two very thin finishing coats directly over the drywall.

The plaster needed for the job is sold ready mixed or in a powder form requiring only the addition of water. It is mixed in the same way as other plasters and has a creamy texture.

Because you are only applying a finishing coat to the drywall board there is no need for thickness guides, except at any external corners (see page 22).

It is a good idea to practice scooping the plaster from the hawk on to the trowel first, using a spare piece of drywall to try your hand at spreading the plaster and making it stick to the board. The technique is to hold the hawk in your left hand (or right if you are left handed) so the top is level and set the trowel blade on edge, so it is at right angles to the top of the hawk. Use the trowel to push some plaster towards the edge of the hawk, scooping it off at the same time as tilting the hawk towards you. The whole is done in one smooth movement.

Dealing with the joints

The first job is to seal the joints between the individual panels of gypsumboard, reinforcing them with perforated paper tape or nylon tape to prevent the plaster cracking. The standard paper tape is available in 2in wide rolls of 50–500 feet.

Cut strips of tape to run the length of each joint, including any horizontal ones, before you begin plastering. They must be exactly the right length and should not overlap or be folded, otherwise the plaster will not grip the wall properly.

To seal the joint, spread a thin layer of plaster, about 4in wide, along it from bottom to top. Hold the trowel so that the blade is at an angle of about 30° to the wall, reducing it as you move up the joint and the plaster on the trowel thins.

While the plaster is still wet, press the tape into it. The easiest way to do this is by draping one end over the blade of the trowel and pressing this into the plaster at the ceiling. Then gently slide the trowel down the plaster, positioning the tape with your other hand. Once the tape is in place, run the trowel carefully up the plaster to make sure it is bedded properly. Treat all the other joints between the panels in the same way.

Finishing the wall

When the taped joints have dried – which should take about 1½ hours – fill in the areas between them with more plaster. Work upwards from the floor, spreading the plaster in thin vertical strips and being careful not to build up ridges at the joint positions. Stop just short of the ceiling and work downwards from there to get a clean, sharp angle.

Unless you are working on a very small area, by the time you have finished putting on the first coat, the area you started on will be ready for the second coat. This should be about ⅛in thick and applied with long, sweeping strokes to eliminate ridges. Start at the bottom corner of the wall and work upwards and along to make one continuous coating.

Allow the plaster to set slightly and then go back over it with a clean trowel to smooth off the surface. Finally, when it has hardened fully, "polish" the surface by splashing clean water on to it with a paintbrush (about 4in wide) then sweep the trowel back and forth lightly. This will give a smooth, matt finish ready for decoration.

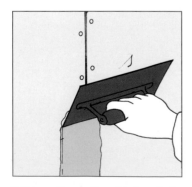

1 Spreading a 4in wide band of plaster, from bottom to top, over the join between sheets of tapered-edge gypsumboard.

2 Bedding joint tape into the plaster with a trowel, working from top to bottom; this reinforces the plaster and stops it cracking.

3 Spreading plaster in thin vertical strips in the bays between taped joints; work from bottom to top to avoid forming ridges.

4 Spread the finishing coat over the entire area with long, sweeping strokes to remove any ridges which may have been formed in the first coat.

PLASTERING MASONRY

To plaster a newly built wall you will not have to do any preparation work to it at all before you fix wooden grounds or metal lath in place.

Then the masonry should be dampened by splashing on clean water with a paintbrush. This will help slow down the rate at which the wall absorbs moisture from the plaster, preventing it from drying out too quickly and possibly cracking.

Applying the floating coat

It is a good idea to practice scooping plaster from the hawk and applying it to the wall before you attempt the job for real. Set the loaded trowel against the wall so that the bottom corner of the blade rests on the ground or bead and the blade is at an angle of about 30° to the wall surface. Move the blade upwards to spread a vertical strip of plaster next to the thickness guide, keeping the blade resting on the guide and gradually reducing its angle as the plaster spreads.

Apply more strips of plaster in the same way, working upwards from the bottom and across the bay adding a good thickness of plaster to the wall.

When the bay is finished, use the long wooden rule to strike it off level with the thickness guides. Place it across the guides and draw it upwards, moving it from side to side in a sawing motion as you go. This will level off the high spots and accentuate the dips. Add more plaster and repeat the process until level.

Before it sets, key the surface for the finishing coat by passing a wooden float, with nails knocked through its face, over the plaster to leave score lines.

Applying the finishing coat

When the floating coat has hardened (it should take about two hours), you can apply the finishing coat. This is done in exactly the same way as plastering wallboard, applying two thin coats of Finish plaster to produce a polished, flat and hard surface.

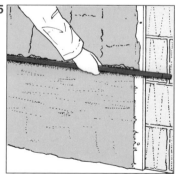

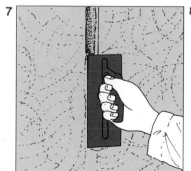
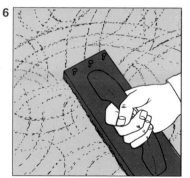

1 Scooping plaster from the hawk; put the trowel into the plaster and scoop forwards and upwards

2 Practising applying paster to the wall; work upwards from waist-height, starting with the trowel at 30 degrees to the wall.

3 As you apply the plaster, tilt the trowel more parallel to the wall surface; keep the hawk close to the wall to catch droppings.

4 Applying the plaster in vertical strips; at the end of each stroke, press the lower edge of the trowel to firm the plaster onto the wall.

5 Ruling off the completed bay; use a straight-edge with a sawing motion to lower any high spots and to show up areas with too little plaster.

6 Scoring the surface to provide a key for the finishing coat; the nails should protrude ⅛in through the float.

7 Filling the gap left after taking off the ground batten; level off with the trowel, flush with the hardened plaster on each side.

8 Applying the finishing coat; work from bottom to top and cover the floating coat with a thin layer; apply a second coat.

9 Polishing the finishing coat; wet the surface sufficiently to remove ridges and marks and polish firmly with a perfectly clean, flat trowel.

DEALING WITH CORNERS

The main problem when plastering corners, whether external or internal, is getting a good, sharp angle. You will face a similar problem at the junction between the wall and ceiling. However, the techniques for dealing with both types of corner are not difficult to master.

Dealing with external corners

There are two forms of guide you can use for forming an external corner: a timber batten or purpose-made metal beading.

The wooden batten is used as a thickness guide for the floating coat then the finishing coat on each wall. Nail it on to one wall so that it projects by the right amount beyond the other and use as a ground for that wall. Then, when the plaster has set, move it round the corner and repeat the process. Any sharp ridges on the apex of the corner should be sliced off with the trowel blade and then the corner rounded off with a block plane or rasp. With wallboard you must tape the angle first.

Two depths of metal beading are available to deal with masonry or gypsumboard-clad walls and they can be fixed in place with plaster or galvanized nails. On wallboard, nails must be used. The beading acts as a ground for the floating coat on masonry walls. Before this hardens, cut back the level to allow for the finish coat. Trowel off flush with beading, leaving the nose exposed to provide a knock-resistant corner.

Dealing with internal corners

For dealing with internal corners, you need a long wood rule. Use this to rule the floating coat outwards from the corner.

After keying the floating coat, cut out the angle by running the corner of the trowel blade up and down it, holding the blade flat against each wall in turn. This will produce a sharp angle. The finish coat should be treated in the same manner. The final job is to hold the short side of the blade against one wall so the long side is just touching the fresh plaster. Hold the blade at 30°–40° and gently run it down the corner.

For finishing corners where both walls have been plastered, use a special V-shaped angle trowel. This produces a constant right angle in the fresh plaster. Load a small amount of plaster onto the angled blade of the trowel and run it lightly down the angle.

1 Reinforcing the external corner of a masonry wall with angle-bead; set it into blobs of plaster, 12in apart.

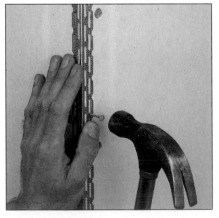

2 Plastering one wall; work away from the corner, using the nose of the bead as a thickness guide.

3 Plastering the adjoining wall in the same way; leave the nose just visible. Score the surface of both walls.

4 Applying the finishing coat, this time covering the nose; round off the corner by running a wet finger along the bead.

5 Securing angle-bead to the internal corner with galvanized nails; nail through the drywall into the stud.

6 Applying a coat of finishing plaster, working away from the corner; the nose should be left visible in this case.

OPENING UP THE SPACE

Rather than wanting more rooms in your house, you may find that you would prefer fewer larger rooms. Some rooms may be too small for their intended use, while others may be too large.

Kitchens are commonly too small for comfort, particularly in older houses, which were not designed for all the equipment we take for granted today. Bathrooms too can often be cramped. Or the rooms generally may feel claustrophobic, and can often be gloomy if they have small windows or are on the shady side of the house.

Many problems of this kind can be overcome by removing part or even the entire wall between two rooms. For example, a kitchen and dining room or a dining room and living room could be combined. Removing the wall between a bedroom and small room, or even making an opening in it will provide more closet space or room for a shower.

Of course, the problem might not be one of having insufficient space in any one room, but rather poor access between rooms. It is not unusual for there to be no direct access between a kitchen and dining room, the route between them being via a hall. Making a doorway in the dividing wall, or even a pass-through, will make life much more bearable and will prevent such things as cooking smells from drifting through the house.

Whether you are making a simple pass-through or taking out an entire wall, the method is basically the same. Before making the opening, a steel, concrete or wooden beam is inserted in the wall to span the opening and support any load on it from above. Then the opening is cut out below this beam and the floor, walls and ceiling are refinished.

Planning the job

The most important aspect of this type of job is planning, since the wall you intend breaking through may contribute to the overall strength of the house and without it, the building may come crashing about your ears. Walls fall into two categories – load-bearing and non-load-bearing – and you must identify which it is before starting work (see page 24).

If you are in any doubt about this stage of the job, consult a structural engineer or architect. You may have to submit plans of the job to your local building department. They will be concerned that you don't breach the Building Code (see page 9) and will pay particular attention as to how you intend supporting the wall above the opening and also – in the case of enlarged rooms – to the amount of light and ventilation the new room will have. If you intend making an opening in one of the exterior walls, you generally must apply for a building permit. Always check your local code before beginning any job.

Other points to bear in mind when considering this kind of work are that you will need to completely redecorate the new large room and you will also have to do something about heating. Previously you could heat two small rooms separately, now you will have to heat one large one and so you may need to upgrade any heating appliances.

Pipe and cable runs in the wall you are to work on should also be dealt with by rerouting them before work begins. If you are only making a doorway or hatch, moving its position slightly may avoid the need to reroute the services.

The job involves a lot of dust and debris, even if you are only making a small opening, so if at all possible remove all of the furnishings from the rooms affected. Cover anything else with dust sheets and lay a thick plastic sheet on the floor on which the debris and rubbish can be collected.

Above: The archway in this wall provides a focal point and leads the eye from the dining area through the living room to the garden.

BRIDGING OPENINGS

The way you tackle the job of making an opening in a wall or removing the wall completely, depends on the type of wall it is and its construction.

A load-bearing wall contributes to the strength of the house by supporting some of its structure: a floor/ceiling, an upstairs wall or part of the roof.

A non-load-bearing wall is simply a dividing partition and its complete removal will have no effect on the rest of the house.

Inspect the floor space above it for signs that it supports the joists, or an upstairs wall. Look in the attic, too, to see if any of the roof framework rests on the wall in question.

All external walls are load-bearing and in general any wall at right-angles to the joists will be load-bearing too. Walls that run parallel to the joists are probably non-load-bearing.

Walls may be of brick, concrete blocks or be wood framed. All three types of construction are used for both load-bearing and non-load-bearing walls.

When you make an opening in a wall, no matter how narrow or wide, you must insert a supporting beam or lintel across the opening to take the load of the structure above, even if it is a non-load-bearing wall. The problem is that even by removing a narrow row of bricks or blocks to make room for the beam will put the structure at risk.

For a narrow opening like a door, the bonding pattern of the bricks or blocks will tend to make the wall above the opening self-supporting (or self-corbelling) and only a small triangular section of masonry will be at risk. This can be removed, the lintel fitted and the masonry replaced.

With a very wide opening, the self supporting tendency will disappear and a wide area of the wall will be liable to collapse. To prevent this happening, you must support the wall (and sometimes the ceiling on either side) temporarily with heavy wood and adjustable props.

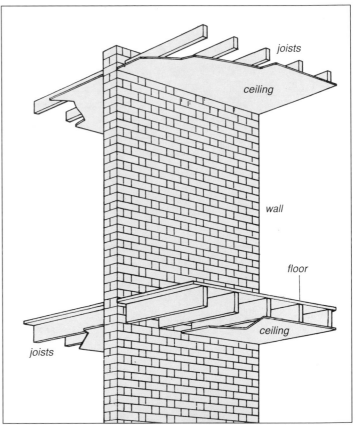

Above: Load-bearing wall – joists run at right-angles to the wall, and the floorboards will be parallel to the surface.

Left: Non load-bearing wall – joists run parallel to the surface.

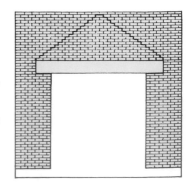

Right: In a narrow opening, the brickwork outside the triangle is self-supporting; a lintel is needed to support the masonry within the triangle and the structure above.

Types of beam

Openings in walls may be spanned by lengths of concrete, steel or wood. Those for fitting over small openings like doors and windows are called lintels; those for spanning wider gaps are called beams. The following are common: Steel Joist – a heavy I or L-shaped girder for spanning very wide gaps in load-bearing walls; Reinforced Concrete Lintel – for internal or solid brick external walls in spans of up to 10ft. Heavy to lift and often cast on the job site, is the Pre-stressed Concrete Lintel – lighter than reinforced concrete lintels but not suitable for load-bearing walls, except in upper floors. For spans of up to 10ft, the wood lintel is used in wood framed walls.

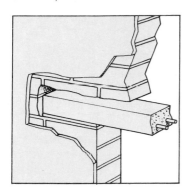

Left: A reinforced-concrete lintel set into a brick wall. To support and distribute its load, a lintel must rest on a bearing at both ends; slot it 9in into the masonry, bed it on a 3:1 mortar mix and fill above and at the ends with mortar.

MAKING A NEW DOORWAY

As with all jobs of this type, making a new doorway requires careful planning. You should also check the requirements of your local building code.

A lintel must be chosen to match the type of wall being cut into (see page 24) and you must select a position for the door that, if possible, will not interfere with existing cable and pipe runs and which should be at least 18in from any corner.

It is possible to buy doors and ready-made frames in a range of standard sizes, and unless you are making the frame, it is best to buy the door and frame first, making the opening to fit it. Make sure its height leaves enough of the wall above the opening for fitting the lintel and the temporary wood supports.

Providing temporary support

With a masonry wall, you must provide temporary support for the wall above the opening and the load it carries while you cut out a slot for the lintel. If the wall supports the joists of the ceiling above, you must also make sure you support the ceiling on both sides of the wall as well.

Support the wall with 6ft lengths of 2 x 4in wood called "needles" – on top of adjustable metal props,

which work like an automobile jack (you can rent these), spaced at 3ft intervals. With a normal sized doorway, you would need only one set centrally above the opening.

To support the ceiling, lengths of 4 × 12in wood are used across the tops of more props. None of the props should be more than 2ft from the wall, and if they are to stand on a wood floor, the feet should be placed on another length of 2 × 4in wood to spread the load.

Marking out the opening

Before marking out the doorway on the wall, use a bricklayer's chisel and hammer to remove patches of plaster roughly where the edges and top of the opening will be. This will allow you to adjust fairly accurately the position of the opening to coincide with the mortar joints, in order to reduce the number of bricks you have to cut through.

Measure up the door frame, adding 2in to its width and 1in to its height to allow for positioning. Using these dimensions, draw an outline of the opening on the wall. Then measure up the lintel – which should be at least 1ft wider than the opening – and add a further 2in to its width for fitting. Draw the outline of the lintel on the wall above the door opening.

Finally, draw the outline of the wood needle centrally above the needle outline. Repeat the outlines on the other side of the wall.

Fitting the needles

Cut the hole for the needle with a hammer and bricklayer's chisel. Slide the needle through so it protrudes equally on both sides of the wall and fit the props beneath it, tightening them to take the load. Both props must be adjusted simultaneously to ensure even support. Then fit the ceiling supports.

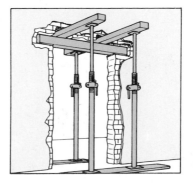

A new wall opening supported by metal jacks bearing onto wooden needles within the opening; stand the jacks on strong planks.

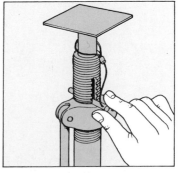

Adjusting a metal jack; with the pin removed, raise the inner tube to the required height, insert the pin and tighten with the handle.

Fitting the lintel

Wearing protective clothing, as described on page 32, (especially the goggles), carefully cut away the plaster from within the lintel outline to expose the masonry below. Remove the bricks or blocks by cutting through their mortar joints and lifting them out. If any above the slot should drop, remove these and keep them for replacement later. Retain any whole bricks from the slot for possible reuse.

Lift the lintel into place, bedding it on mortar (3 parts soft sand: 1 part masonry cement) laid on the "bearings" at each end of the slot. It is best to get the help of an assistant with lifting the lintel, especially when lifting weights above the head. Make sure the lintel is level and, if necessary, pack it out below the ends with tiles or slates.

Finally, fill any spaces around the lintel with more mortar and replace any bricks or blocks that may have dropped out at the slot-cutting stage. If the wall is constructed of blocks, bring the lintel up to the height of the adjacent blocks by laying a course of bricks on top, and mortering them in place.

Cutting the opening

Leave the mortar to set for at least 24 hours, and preferably 48. Then remove the needle and wood supports. Fill the needle holes with brick offcuts and mortar. Lever off the baseboard and place it to one side for cutting down later.

Remove the plaster inside the outline of the opening to expose all the masonry below. Using a light sledge hammer and bolster chisel, cut this out by chiseling through the mortar joints, carefully working down the wall one course at a time. Because of the bonding pattern used, you will find that on alternate courses you will have to cut through bricks at the sides of the opening. Do this as you come to them, driving the chisel into their faces and levering them out from below to leave a straight edge to the opening. Remove all the bricks from the opening.

Trim off the masonry flush with a solid floor, or just below a wooden one. In the latter case, join the two floors by screwing battens to the joists then fit a piece of plywood or short pieces of floor-board on top to neaten and close the gap.

1 Removing a brick to enable the prop needle to be inserted above the position of the lintel.

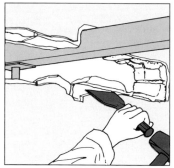

2 With the props in place to support the brickwork above, removing bricks to make way for the lintel.

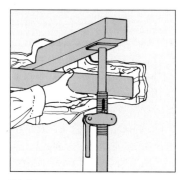

3 Lifting the lintel onto its bed of mortar; ensure that it has a bearing of 9in each side of the opening.

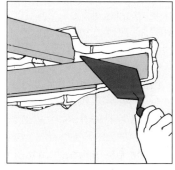

4 Filling around the lintel with mortar; this must be allowed to cure for at least 24 hours before removing the props.

5 Chipping away the plaster within the marked lines beneath the lintel.

6 Removing the brickwork to form the opening; cut at right-angles through any protruding bricks to leave a clean edge.

7 Screwing a metal frame-tie to the door-frame; six ties are needed in all and must lie between mortar joints in the sides of the opening.

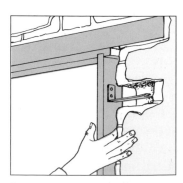

8 Fitting the frame tie into a pocket cut in the brickwork; set the tie in mortar and fill the gap above it with brick fillets and mortar.

Fitting the frame

The frame can be held in place with either galvanized metal ties mortared to the wall, or by screws and wall plugs. If ties are to be used, you need three per side. Cut recesses in the sides of the opening for the ties. If you intend screwing the frame to the wall, drill screw clearance holes in it and offer it up so these can be marked on the wall. Drill and plug the holes.

Set the frame in place, packing out the sides as necessary with wood offcuts to set them vertical. Then either fill the tie recesses with mortar and brick offcuts or insert the screws.

Fill in the gaps round the frame with more mortar and offcuts and trowel a thin layer of mortar over any exposed masonry at the sides and top before refinishing the plaster.

Finally, nail lengths of moulding around the frame, mitering the corners, and trim and refit the base boards to the base of the wall.

Doorways in stud partitions

To put a doorway in a stud partition, first expose the framework below the skin of the partition. Find the stud positions on each side of the proposed opening by tapping the surface and probing with a bradawl. Draw in the stud positions on the surface and another line between them to mark the height of the door frame plus an allowance for the wood lintel.

Cut along this outline with a keyhole saw continuing the cut through the skin across the top of any studs or bracing you come across. Lever off the skin to expose the framework and the back of the other skin. Remove the latter in the same way.

Cut out all the framework within the opening and then make up two short "trimmer" studs to support the lintel. Nail the trimmer studs to the original studs on each side of the opening and the lintel to the tops of the trimmer studs. Nail through the lintel into the base of any cut stud.

If the door frame is narrower than the distance between the trimmer studs, fit an intermediate between the lintel and sole plate, linking it with short braces to one of the trimmer studs.

Cut out the section of sole plate across the bottom of the opening and fit the door frame as described on page 16. Finish the partition by nailing on gypsum-board and applying a skim coat of plaster over the top, see page 20.

MAKING A HATCHWAY

A hatchway between a kitchen and dining room can be extremely useful, and you may wish to consider installing one should you have to block off a redundant doorway, or to suit other remodeling plans. Plan its position carefully so that it coincides with a work surface in the kitchen and something like a worktop or small table in the dining room so that there will be somewhere to place dishes and plates, for example.

The method for making a pass-through is basically the same as that for making a doorway (see page 26), except that the opening is not continued to the floor. In a wood framed partition, a wood sill piece is needed between the studs on each side of the opening.

The pass-through can be left open with plastered edges and a wood sill, screwed across the bottom or a wooden lining frame can be fitted to take hinged or sliding doors, or some form of roller blind to give the maximum amount of privacy, and also to prevent cooking smells, for example, from drifting through.

A new doorway set in an existing door to form a pass through between kitchen and dining room.

A pass through between living room and kitchen/dining room, set into a wall and closed off with a roller blind.

BLOCKING REDUNDANT DOORWAYS

There are two methods you can use for blocking off a redundant doorway: you can fit a wood framework around the inside and panel it with wallboard on both sides, or you can use bricks or lightweight building blocks if the floor is solid. In each case, plaster is used to finish it off.

Glass shelves form a light barrier.

Alternatively, consider whether you can put it to some other use such as paneling in the back and filling the recess with shelves.

Removing the old frame

To remove the old door and frame, unscrew the door hinges, lift the door away and lever off the molding. The lining frame may be fixed by masonry nails, screws or metal ties cemented into the brickwork. You should be able to lever it free, but if not, cut through its fixings by working a saw blade between the back of the frame and the wall.

Paneling with wallboard

If you are filling an opening in a stud partition, the supporting framework should be made of wood to match the framework of the partition – usually 2 × 3 or 4in lumber. On the other hand, if paneling a

masonry wall, you might need two separate frames of something like 2in sq wood to panel each side flush.

The frame should comprise a head plate, sole plate, two upright studs and a central brace. Toe-nail these together and to the insides of the opening, making sure the frame is set back from the face of the wall to allow for the thickness of the skimmed wallboard.

Nail a panel of wallboard to each side of the frame, and to prevent the skim coat shrinking back from the edges, nail lengths of metal lath around the join. Apply a skim coat of finish (see page 20) and when the plaster has hardened, fit a length of new baseboard across the opening.

Filling in with masonry

To fill the opening with bricks or concrete blocks, you must tie the new masonry to the old. The easiest method is to hammer 6in masonry nails half-way into the side of the opening to correspond with the mortar joints of alternate courses of the new bricks which will eventually be buried in the mortar.

Lay the bricks or blocks in the normal overlapping fashion and point all the mortar joints flush with the face of the masonry when finished.

Finally, apply floating and finish coats of plaster as described on page 21, using the surrounding original plaster as a thickness guide.

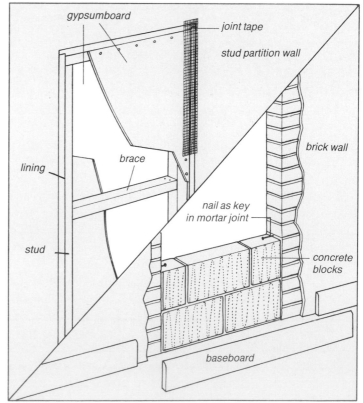

Two methods of filling a doorway.

CUTTING AN EXTERNAL DOORWAY

The positioning and installation of external doors is subject to the requirements of your local building code, so make the necessary applications to your local building department first (see page 9).

Fitting the lintel

Temporary support for the wall must be provided by 3in sq needles on top of adjustable metal props. To fit the needles, remove a whole brick from the outer layer and drill through the inner layer at the corners of the opening. Use the holes as a guide for cutting out the masonry from the inner layer. Insert the needles and tighten the props.

Draw the outline of the lintel on the inside wall and cut out the plaster and masonry from within. Drill the corners of the outer layer and remove the masonry. Fit the lintel on mortar bearings packed out with tiles or slates to set it level. Fill all round the inner portion of the lintel with mortar and rebuild any brickwork above it. Similarly rebuild the outer brickwork in the existing bond or stand the bricks on end to form a "sodier" arch.

Cutting the opening

When the mortar has set, remove the needles and brick up the holes. Then cut out the opening for the door frame – to fit the size of the frame.

Remove the bricks down to floor level, cutting through the protrud-bricks of the inner layer, on solid walls but removing whole bricks from the outer layer to give a toothed appearance. Square up the toothed outer layer by fitting cut bricks in place so that their "finished" ends are outermost.

Fitting the frame

Toe-nail the frame together before inserting it in the opening. Tack a length of flashing material to the underside of the sill, covering the nail heads with a bituminous sealant.

Fix the frame in the opening with screws and wallplugs, packing the sides to make them vertical. Fill gaps on the inside with mortar; apply caulking around the frame on the outside to keep out water.

The door sill should overhang the brickwork slightly and is best fitted with a metal weather bar, which is set in caulk. Once the frame is in place, hang the door and finish the internal surfaces with plaster.

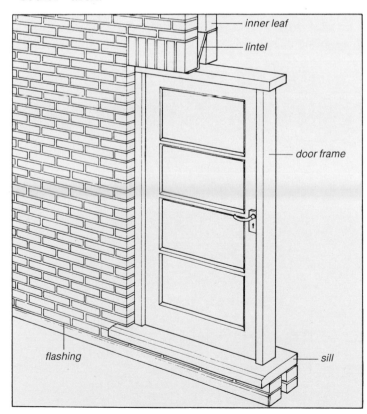

1 Cutting out bricks to form the opening; unlike internal doorways, the bricks are not cut flush at the sides.

2 Filling the gaps with half-bricks; spread mortar on top of the whole brick and butter the end and top of the half-brick.

3 After recessing and screwing one leaf of the hinge to the door, mark, recess and screw the free leaf to the door-jamb.

4 Fitting the door-frame to the wall; drill through the frame into the brickwork and secure with frame-fixing plugs and screws.

A doorway in an external solid brick wall. The galvanized steel lintel must be installed so that it slopes downwards towards the outer leaf of the wall. The DPC under the sill should link up with the DPC in the wall at each side of the door.

Labels in diagram: inner leaf, lintel, door frame, flashing, sill

ENLARGING A ROOM

The techniques for removing a wall between two rooms to turn them into one large, through-room are essentially the same as those needed to make a new doorway or a pass-through but on a larger scale.

However, if the wall is load-bearing much more of the structure of the house will be at risk from collapse, so you must take particular care to ensure that you provide temporary support for any loads carried by the wall before you start to remove it and, just as importantly, that there is adequate permanent support when finished. This means finding out if the floor joists of the room above rest upon it and also if the same wall continues upwards to form a dividing wall on the floor above, for example. This is where you may find it necessary to check first with a professional contractor.

If there is no continuation wall above and the floor joists simply rest on top of the wall, you can remove it completely, using stout wood planks and adjustable props to bear the weight of the joists from below while the supporting beam (see page 24) is set in place. However, if there is a continuation of the wall, you must leave a margin at ceiling level to allow for the insertion of wooden needles at 3ft intervals.

Ceiling joists at right-angles to the wall must be supported by props under planks, spaced at 3ft intervals.

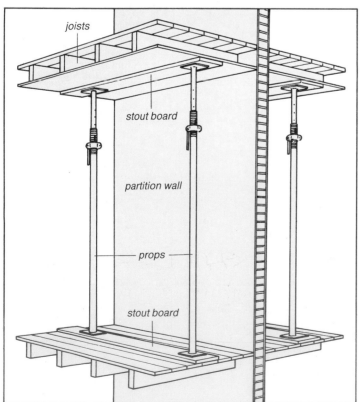

Choosing a supporting beam

As already mentioned, it is normal for wide spans of this sort to be supported by a steel beam but long beams can be very heavy and you might find it easier to use a steel angle instead. This will be lighter and only good for shorter spans depending on the size.

You could also use a reinforced concrete beam or a pre-stressed concrete beam (the lighter of the two). But both will only cope with spans of 10ft so they are only really suitable for narrow rooms.

In any event you may have to gain approval from your local Building Inspector for the way you intend to tackle the job, and this includes your choice of beam. If you are not sure of the best type to use always take professional advice or check with your local Building Code.

Whatever type of beam you choose, it will still be heavy and you will need helpers to lift it into position. You will also need enough extra adjustable props to support it at 3ft intervals while you mortar it in place.

Lintel supported on the stubs of the original wall (top left), and on piers adjacent to the wall (bottom left). Inset: section down onto a lintel showing how it rests with its front face flush with the padstone and supporting pier.

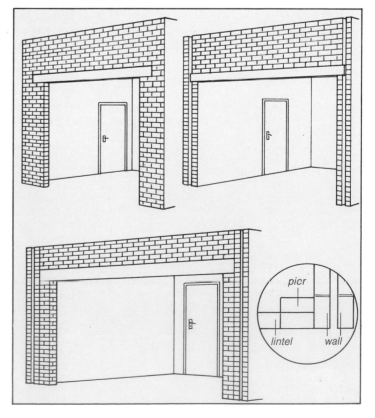

Creating the bearings

The ends of the beam must rest on bearings that are 6 to 9in wide, and because of the heavy loads carried it is usual to support the beam on concrete "pad-stones" (concrete blocks are ideal). This helps to spread the load evenly across the bearings.

As an alternative to a concrete padstone, you could use a heavy steel plate, or one or two courses of a strong brick; normal facing bricks would crumble under the weight.

Supporting the bearings

The bearings must have substantial support below them to cope with the loads imposed on them from above and the way you arrange this support can take several forms. It is something that the Building Inspector will pay particular attention to.

A common method of supplying support for the bearings is to build brick columns or piers at each end of the span, toothing every second course into the brickwork of the adjoining walls.

Such piers must have substantial foundations of their own and this usually means digging down into the ground below, putting in a layer of well compacted gravel and pouring a thick layer of concrete on top. The exact requirements will be specified by your local Code which should be checked at the beginning.

Once the foundation has hardened, you can begin building the footings of the piers, remembering to set flashing in one of the mortar joints level with the flashing of the existing walls. This should be just below the level of the floor. If the floor is solid concrete, it should have a damp-proof membrane in it and you must take steps to see that your new flashing and the membrane are sealed together.

In some cases you may be allowed to use a course of engineering bricks as a flashing.

When the pier has been built, it is topped with mortar and the padstone set in place and leveled.

If the wall you are breaking through is a solid 8in thick wall, you may be able to leave short stubs of the wall projecting into the room to act as piers for the ends of the beam. However, you will need to check with your local Building Code to be satisfied that the original wall has substantial enough foundations. Remember, the weight carried by the wall, which was spread evenly along the length of its foundations will, on removal of the wall, be concentrated on two much smaller patches.

The mortar of the old wall should be in good condition, too. If it is loose or crumbly, rake out all the joints and repoint them with fresh mortar.

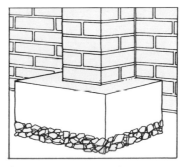

1 Piers are supported on concrete padstones, cast on top of compacted gravel.

2 Wear stout gloves, overalls, face-mask and goggles when knocking down masonry; and a helmet when working overhead.

3 Lifting the lintel on to a bed of mortar on top of the supporting brick pier; assistance will be needed for this operation.

4 Wedging the lintel on the pier with a tile; slate or slips of brick may equally be used.

Ceiling joists parallel to the wall are propped with needles passed through the wall above the level of the lintel.

If the walls running across the ends of the beam are load-bearing, it may be possible to cut directly into them to form bearings. In this situation a longer than normal padstone should be used to spread the load sideways, or it may be necessary to add some extra strengthening by toothing-in a shallow pier.

If you decide to construct piers, you can save some of the cost of renting adjustable jacks by building the piers before the bulk of the wall is removed. Cut out enough masonry from each end of the wall to allow room for the piers to be built, leaving enough of the wall in place to carry the load without risk of collapse. Then when the piers have been completed and hardened off, you can rent the necessary equipment and begin demolition.

Removing the wall

Having arranged temporary support with planks, needles and props and decided how you are going to tackle the job of providing bearings, start to remove the masonry from the wall.

First draw the outline of the opening on the wall with a pencil and long straightedge. Remove the plaster from within the outlines using a light sledge and bricklayer's chisel. This will be very dusty work, so it is essential to empty both rooms of all furnishings and seal any doorways by pinning thick plastic sheets or old blankets over them. This will prevent the dust spreading to the rest of the house, Sprinkle the debris with water from a houseplant sprayer to settle the dust. Wear safety goggles, a facemask, thick gloves and stout boots when hacking off the plaster or removing the masonry.

With the masonry of the wall exposed, begin chopping out the bricks or blocks by cutting into their mortar joints and levering them upwards with the blade of the chisel. Try to keep as many bricks as possible in one piece because they are always useful to have around for other jobs.

Nevertheless there will still be a massive amount of rubble to dispose of and one way is to put it into stout plastic sacks as you go and take these to a local dump when the job is finished. Alternatively, you could rent a small rubbish container, which is much more convenient. If you intend leaving it in the road, check with your Sanitation Department since many will not allow this unless they have given you prior authorization. You may also have to ensure it is properly lit at night to avoid accidents.

Unlike making a new doorway, where you cut a slot for the lintel first, fit it and then remove the masonry below, when making a through room with its associated heavy beam this is not really feasible, since it would be very difficult to lift in place and support. You must make the complete opening while the load above is still supported by the temporary props. It is essential to have all the necessary tools, equipment and materials to hand so that you can proceed quickly with the job.

At floor level, either trim the masonry off flush with a solid floor, or just below a wooden one. In the latter case, take care not to break through any water proofing membrane.

If there is a difference of level between the floors of the two rooms, either build a wooden step or cast a concrete one *in situ*.

Positioning the beam

With the masonry removed, you can make the bearings. Lifting the beam into place will be heavy work so it is as well to do a little preparation beforehand. To avoid the need for lifting the beam from floor level to the ceiling in one go, support it on trestles or pairs of stepladders, setting it so that you can get hold of it easily.

Set the coarse adjustment of the jack posts that will support the beam so that they can be set in place quickly and the fine adjustment made without fuss.

Lift the beam into place on the capstones and check that it is square across the room by taking measurements from nearby fixed points. Set the jack posts in place and tighten them until the beam comes up tight against the joists or masonry above. Check that the beam is completely level and make any fine adjustments with the posts.

At this stage you can remove the posts holding the joists, but leave any needles in place.

Finishing the bearings

Trowel a layer of mortar between the top of the capstone and the underside of the beam and then tap pieces of slate into place to wedge the beam tightly upwards. You may need to insert two or even three pieces. Do the same at the other bearing, making sure it forms as tight a wedge as possible.

Finish off by pointing more mortar round the ends of the beam and capstone. If it is set on bearings cut into the end walls, fill the cavities around the ends of the beam with whole bricks or offcuts and more mortar, pointing it neatly.

With the bearings finished, check along the top of the beam to make sure it is fully supporting the joists or masonry above. If there are any gaps they must be wedged out too. In the case of masonry, use mortar

Plastering over a steel box beam with metal lathing plaster; when this has hardened, complete the job with a coat of finishing plaster.

A floor-standing structural brick arch. A semicircular framework is used to support the bricks during construction and serve as a template for the shape. The bricks may be cut to wedge shapes and laid with uniform mortar joints, or be uncut and with tapered joints (a rough arch). At the sides of the arch, where the headroom is limited, cabinets have been used here to form a central passageway.

and more slate wedges. If it is a wood floor, drive slates between the beam and any joists that are not otherwise supported.

Finishing off

Allow the mortar to harden for at least two days before removing the jack posts from below the beam together with any needles and their posts. Fill the needle holes with brick offcuts and mortar, then make good the ceiling, adjacent walls and floor.

If you have used a steel beam, clad this in a material that will protect it from fire: do not leave it exposed. The usual method is to clad the beam with gypsumboard on a wooden framework nailed to wedges hammered into the sides of the beam.

The corners of the gypsumboard should be taped or fitted with metal corner beads and finished as described on page 29.

Concrete beams can be directly plastered over, their surfaces being rough enough to provide a key for the floating and finish coats.

When the beam has been plastered, finish the piers as well, using battens or special beads to form the corners as described on page 29. (Beading is probably best since the piers project into the room slightly and are, therefore, more likely to be knocked.)

Finally, cut the baseboards to fit around the base of each pier.

Dealing with a non-load-bearing wall

If the wall is of the non-load-bearing variety, the job will be much simpler since there is no need to fit a beam.

With a masonry wall, simply hack off the plaster and remove it brick by brick or block by block from the ceiling down. Cut out any metal ties holding the partition to the end walls, or cut through any bricks or blocks that have been toothed into them. At floor level, trim the masonry off flush – it may just sit on top of the floor anyway.

Replace the ceiling, if necessary, by cutting back to the nearby joists and nailing on a fresh strip of gypsumboard. Finish it off with a skim coat of plaster and repair any damage to the walls.

If the wall is a wood-framed stud partition, simply lever off the cladding and prise apart or unscrew the frame. Fill any holes in the adjoining walls and redecorate.

• CHECKPOINT •

MESH ARCH FORMERS

One of the problems with taking out a wall between two rooms to make a through-room is that the beam and its supporting piers remain as clear evidence of what has been done. The same applies if you remove a door and frame from their opening to make an open plan access point between two rooms. These functional pieces of the structure can be disguised and made to look more decorative by forming them into curved archways.

Construction

There are many ways in which you can construct archways from scratch, using a basic framework of sawn wood clad with hardboard, plywood, drywall or imitation bricks, but probably the easiest is to use prefabricated galvanized steel mesh arch formers. These are fixed in place at the top of the opening and plastered to match the adjoining walls.

Mesh arch formers usually come in four pieces, each piece being half of the face of one side of the arch and half of the associated area of soffit. In this way they can be trimmed down to fit narrow walls, or widened by the addition of extra soffit strips. They are available in a variety of shapes and sizes for spans of up to 10ft. Some one-piece versions are also available.

The faces of the prefabricated mesh panels are usually extended at the edges to form mounting flanges which sit flat against the face of the wall. The formers are secured by driving galvanized masonry nails through the flanges into the wall or by pushing the flanges into dabs of plaster.

If you intend to disguise a newly fitted beam with arch formers, they should be installed before you plaster either the beam or the piers. If you want to improve the look of an existing opening, you will have to cut away a margin of plaster so that the mounting flanges of the formers will sit back flush against the wall.

Instead of using Bonding plaster for the floating coat, the mesh arch formers should be given a backing coat of Metal Lathing plaster. This hardens to leave a rough finish ready for the application of thin layers of Finish plaster. Rule the finish layer level with any surrounding original plaster.

1 Cutting the soffit of an arch section to width after holding it in position and marking the wall thickness on the soffit.

2 Fixing the arch section to the wall with masonry nails; fix expanded metal to a wooden lintel before plastering.

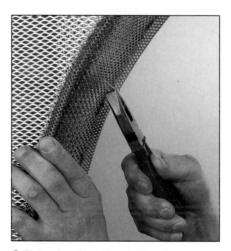

3 Fixing together the soffits of two sections with twists of galvanized wire passed through the mesh.

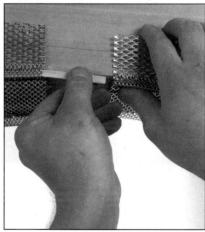

4 Joining adjacent sections with plastic strip pushed into the angle of the mesh and secured with self-tapping screws.

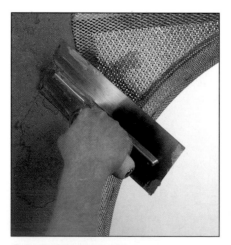

5 Applying metal lathing plaster to the face of the arch and adjoining masonry where the plaster has been cut back.

6 Applying plaster to the soffit; rule off flush with the surrounding plaster and apply a finishing coat.

ENLARGING A WINDOW

In remodeling your living space you may wish to enlarge a window, either to let in more light or ventilation, by installing an opening window to replace a fixed one.

Window types and materials

Modern windows come in a wide choice of styles in wood metal or plastic. They can be simple fixed panes or they can open with either top-hinged, side-hinged, pivotting, horizontally-sliding or vertically-sliding sections. The tendency is to go for large, uninterrupted panes of glass, but if your house is old you can still buy windows made up of small panes to give it a period look.

Despite the fact that it needs regular maintenance, wood is the most popular material for window frames and offers the widest choice of styles and sizes.

Steel windows are functional in appearance but can suffer considerably from rust if not looked after. Aluminum windows, too, can suffer from corrosion due to the atmosphere, especially in coastal areas.

On the face of it, plastic would seem to be ideal for window frames, being largely maintenance free. However, it is not easy to paint (and is intended not to be), which means that you are stuck with the manufacturer's color, and if this is white you may find it yellows with age.

How frames are fixed

Wooden window frames are normally held in place by galvanized metal ties cemented into the brickwork at the sides of the opening, by nails or screws driven into wooden wedges set in the brickwork, or by screws and wallplugs. Metal-framed windows may be held by metal brackets or be fitted to hardwood frames, which in turn are screwed into the opening.

Plastic frames are treated in the same way.

What the job involves

Assuming that you are going to fit a larger window frame in place of the original, you must provide temporary support for the wall (with needles and jack posts) while you remove the old frame and lintel. This should be either concrete or steel so that both leaves of the wall are supported. For a solid wall, fit a concrete lintel to the inner leaf and, at the same time, form a curved soldier arch over the top of the window in the outer leaf.

With the lintel in place, cut out the brickwork for the larger frame. Prepare the edges of the opening, prop the frame in position and nail, screw or cement it in place. The final job is to seal around the edges with mortar and caulk.

Removing the old frame

To make the frame lighter and easier to handle, first remove any opening sections and then carefully remove all the glass.

Cut out the mortar seal at the edges of the frame with a flat chisel and run a screwdriver round the gap to locate the fixings. Cut through them with a saw inserted in the keyhole.

Having cut through or released the fixings, lever the frame out with a stout bar or knock it out with a length of wood and a light sledge hammer.

Cutting through the metal frame ties of a window with a hacksaw blade held in a handle after cutting away the caulk beading.

Remove sashes, or casements, and fixed glazing from the frame before easing it out; cut and remove in pieces if necessary.

Apart from increasing the area of view and the amount of light which enters a room, a picture window or patio doors can add an extra dimension to a room. Here the floor tiles and paving slabs make the garden feel like an extension of the dining room.

FITTING A NEW LINTEL

With the wall above the window opening supported by stout wooden needles and adjustable jacks, and the old window frame taken out you can remove the old lintel and brickwork from above the opening.

Remove the bricks from the outer layer first. These may be laid in horizontal courses across the lintel or they may be set vertically. If the house is old, they may form a self-supporting segmental arch.

Cut through the mortar joints with a bricklayer's chisel to remove the bricks, making a gradually tapering, stepped opening up to the level of the wooden needle above. This will prevent any brickwork from falling while working on the opening.

Removing the bricks from the outer leaf of the wall will expose the face of the load bearing lintel set in the inner leaf. You should remove this next.

From inside the house, hack off the plaster above the window opening to expose the inner face of the lintel and the brickwork above it. Again, cut out the bricks to form a stepped opening up to the level of the needle. Then cut into the mortar joints at each end of the lintel, working along the top, ends and underneath. Use a stout bar to lever the ends of the lintel upwards to finally release them. Then get some help to lift the lintel from its bearings in the wall.

Do not allow any rubble to fall into any cavity within the thickness of the wall. It may lodge and form a bridge for moisture to cross from the outer skin to the inner and cause damp patches on the inner wall.

Fitting the new lintel

Measure up the new lintel and draw its outline on the inside of the wall centered over the new window position. Remember, the new lintel should be at least 6in wider at each side of the window opening to provide decent-sized bearings. Also, allow an extra 1in at each end and on the depth to provide enough space to manoeuvre the lintel into position.

Cut straight down through the plaster along the outline with the bricklayer's chisel to provide a cutting guide and then hack off the plaster within the outline.

Go on to remove the bricks exposed by the removal of the plaster, again cutting through the mortar joints in an effort to keep as many bricks in one piece as possible. Clean up the bearing openings and make sure their surfaces are flat and level.

Whether you are using a steel or concrete lintel, you will need some help to lift it into place.

Trowel a layer of mortar onto each bearing and lift the lintel into place, setting it centrally over the opening. Check that the lintel is flush with the inner face and outer layer of the wall.

Hold a level against the underside of the lintel and check that it is horizontal. If necessary, correct this by packing pieces of tile or slate beneath the ends. When level, fill the gaps round the ends of the lintel with more mortar and brick offcuts, pointing the joints neatly flush with the surrounding brickwork.

Then replace the brickwork of the inner layer above the lintel, working upwards towards the needle and copying the original brickwork bond.

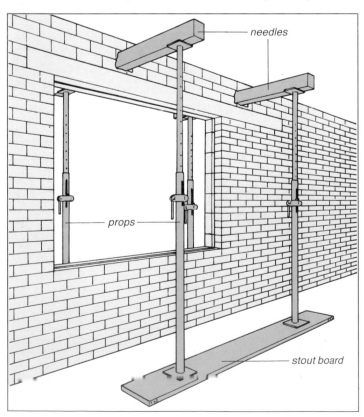

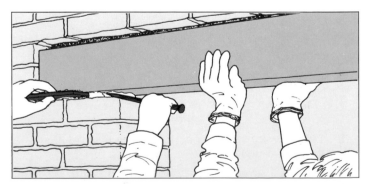

Left: New longer lintel installed in outer leaf of cavity wall, using props and needles to support the brickwork above the opening.

Above: Packing up with piece of tile while assistant supports the weight of the lintel; leverage from a mason's chisel assists in this operation.

ENLARGING THE OPENING

Having set the new lintel in place and re-finished the brickwork of the inner leaf above it, you can cut out the brickwork at the sides of the opening and, if necessary, across the base. First, draw the outline of the new opening on both sides of the wall, making it about 1in wider and deeper than the actual frame dimensions to give a fitting tolerance.

Removing the brickwork

External walls comprise two layers of bricks; each layer should be treated separately, working in from each side of the wall.

If the wall is a solid one produce a square edge along the opening outline on the inner layer by cutting through bricks where necessary. Always remove complete bricks even if they project beyond the outline. This gives a toothed effect to the edge.

If the base outline runs through the center of a course of bricks, remove the course completely; you can make up the difference later.

Finishing the opening

Replace the outer layer at the sides of the opening by mortaring cut bricks into the toothed sections so that their cut ends are innermost.

Next, replace the area of wall above the window, laying the bricks on the lintel and copying the original brickwork bond for strength and appearance. In a solid wall, you can create a curved, self-supporting soldier arch by setting a wooden framework in the opening on which the bricks of the arch are laid. Then the surrounding courses are fitted round the arch and the mortar left to set for a couple of days before removal of the formwork.

Fitting the frame

The frame must sit squarely in the opening; if it is twisted, you may have problems in opening and closing the window and the glass will be under stress and may shatter at the slightest vibration.

In a solid wall you can set the frame: flush with the outer face with its sill overhanging the edge; in the center of the opening with narrow reveals on each side; or flush with the inner face with a sub-sill at the bottom to throw water clear of the wall.

When the frame is set forward in the opening, the sides and top of the reveal are plastered and a wooden or tiled window board set across the bottom. When set at the back, it is normal to trim around the inside of the frame with molding.

1 Marking outline of opening on wall; allow 1in fitting tolerance above frame dimensions.

2 Chipping off the plaster using a mason's chisel and light sledge hammer.

3 Cutting out brickwork to new width of opening; work downwards, do not cut bricks.

4 Toothing out brickwork (on inner leaf of a solid wall, cut bricks to leave a square edge).

5 Removing concrete sub-sill (if present) after cutting back sides of opening.

6 Building up base of opening to within one brick-height of frame; fill in edges with half bricks.

7 Building a soldier course of bricks above opening.

8 Filling in above soldier course with whole bricks; use wedge-shaped cut bricks above the arch.

Fixing the frame

The simplest method of securing the frame is with frame fixings, a hefty screw and long plastic wall plug, but you can also use conventional wallplugs and screws, wooden wedges or metal frame ties. With each type, wedge the frame in the opening with wood offcuts so that it is set squarely in place, while the fixings are marked and made.

With screws and plugs, clearance holes must first be drilled in the frame and the hole positions on the wall marked through these. The holes are drilled and plugged and the frame fitted.

Wooden wedges are tapped into slots cut in the mortar joints and the frame nailed to the wedges. Metal frame ties also fit into slots in the joints, being screwed to the frame and mortared in place.

In all cases, you must leave a $\frac{1}{8}$in gap between the top of the frame and the underside of the lintel to allow for any settlement of the structure.

Leave the packing pieces in place and fill the gaps at the sides with mortar, leaving it about $\frac{1}{8}$in below the level of the frame face. Fill this gap with caulk when the mortar has set. Use caulking to fill the gap between the lintel and frame also. If there is a gap below the frame, fill this with bricks and mortar, splitting the bricks lengthways if necessary.

Making a sub-sill

Make a sub-sill from wood screwed or nailed in place, or a double layer of tiles set on a sloping bed of mortar.

Another way is to cast a concrete sill *in situ*, making up a wooden formwork "tray" nailed to the wall. The sill should overlap the edge of the bricks by no more than 1in and you can form a drip channel (to prevent rainwater trickling under the sill) along the bottom edge by pinning a length of waxed cord (sash window cord will do) in the bottom of the tray. The

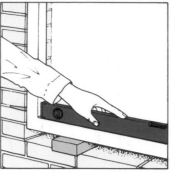

3 Checking that the sill is horizontal using a level; make any necessary adjustment by moving the wooden packing.

4 Checking that the frame is vertical; adjust by tapping with the handle of a hammer.

5 Securing the frame by hammering 4in cut-nails through the frame into the wedges; recheck levels after each fixing.

6 Bricking up under the frame after completing the fixings and removing the timber packing; use bricks split lengthways if necessary.

1 Fitting a timber wedge into a slot cut in a mortar joint; fit wedges near the top and bottom, and in between for tall windows.

2 Wedging the frame in position with wooden blocks; leave $\frac{1}{8}$in gap between the frame and the lintel and later fill with caulking.

top of the lintel should slope downwards so angle the sides for this. Also provide reinforcement by setting steel rods in holes drilled in the brickwork.

Mix the concrete from 4 parts sand: 1 part cement and pour it into the form. Agitate the mix to compact it and remove air bubbles and draw it off level with the top of the form. Leave the concrete for at least 24 hours before removing the formwork.

Alternative frame fixings

The frame fixing is much simpler to use and is ideal for securing wooden members to masonry. It comprises a hefty screw and a long plastic wallplug.

To use, wedge the frame in its opening and drill holes for the fixings right through it and into the wall. Without removing the frame, tap the plug and screw combination through the frame and into the wall, finally tightening the screw for a secure fixing.

Frame fixings are supplied in various lengths to hold wood thicknesses up to 3$\frac{3}{8}$in. Another development of this is the hammer fixing, which is used in the same way, but set by driving a ridged, countersunk pin into the expanding plug.

CHAPTER 2

FLOORS, CEILINGS AND STAIRCASES

In remodeling projects, such as attic conversions and built-on
room extensions, it is inevitable that floors, ceilings and,
maybe, staircases become involved in the major construction
work and may need repairing or entirely renewing.
The following chapter illustrates the various techniques used in
laying wooden floors, casting solid floors, replacing and
plastering ceilings, installing and repairing wooden staircases
— including staircase kits. These are readily available in
different period styles and, despite their complex-looking
structure, are relatively easy to fix.

FLOORING

While the upper floors of a house will always be constructed of wood, the ground floor may be made of wood or it may be of solid concrete.

Suspended wooden floors

All wood floors are based on the same method of construction with minor differences. They all have a supporting framework of wooden beams called joists onto which are nailed wooden boards or plywood panels and may have a plain or decorative finish.

The joists of wooden ground floors are supported at their end – and sometimes at one or two points in between – or additional wood beams known as "wall plates". These, in turn rest on the tops of low brick "sleeper" walls. These are not solid, but are laid in honeycomb fashion with spaces between the bricks to allow the air to circulate below the floor to prevent condensation and rot forming. For the same reason, vents are usually fitted at the base of the external walls and must always be kept clear. Slates or strips of flexible flashing material are laid between the wall plates and sleeper walls to prevent damp attacking the wood.

Sometimes the joists are laid on top of individual bricks set on the ground. Upstairs, the joists are also supported by wall plates but these are held by metal brackets called joist hangers, which are cemented into the walls. Sometimes the joist ends may be set in sockets between the bricks, with a metal plate below to spread the load through the wall.

Solid concrete floors

Most modern houses have solid ground floors. These comprise of a layer of compacted gravel on top of which is a 4in layer of concrete called the subfloor. A damp-proof membrane bitumen or thick plastic is laid next and is carried up and down the wall to link with the flashing around the base of the house.

A thin layer of mortar can be laid on top of the membrane which will provide a level surface for most types of flooring.

Wooden floor faults

Over the years a wooden floor can suffer considerably from wear and tear. The joists may warp or sag, boards may shrink to open up gaps through which draughts whistle, or they may become loose or damaged. The whole structure may be further weakened by woodworm or rot. Fortunately, many of the minor problems can be cured easily, although serious rot or insect attack may mean complete replacement and should be dealt with by a specialist.

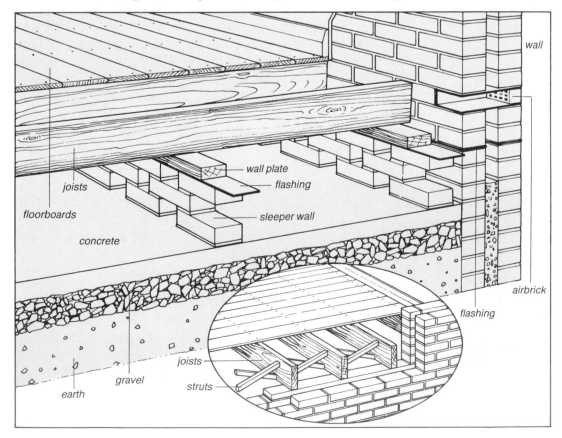

Suspended wooden ground floor; the joists are supported on wall-plates which in turn rest on flashing over open-structure sleeper walls. *Inset:* upper floor joists are stiffened with herringbone struts.

Creaking floorboards

Probably the most common fault with a wooden floor is creaking floorboards due to the fixings working loose. The cure is simple: either drive the nails back in or replace them with longer nails or screws. Punch nail heads below the surface and countersink the screw heads.

Curing gaps between boards

Gaps of less than ¼in can be filled with papier-mâché, which you can make yourself. Half fill a bucket with small pieces of torn, soft white paper, gradually adding boiling water while you pound the paper into a thick paste. Allow it to cool and stir in enough cellulose wallpaper paste to make a thick mixture. Add wood stain to match the color of the boards.

When the papier-mâché is quite cold, force it between the boards with a filling knife, leaving it slightly proud of the surface. Leave it for at least 48 hours then sand smooth.

Fill wider gaps with softwood fillets: cut the fillets fractionally wider than the gaps they are to fill, using a backsaw. The fillets should be fractionally deeper than the floorboards: that is, about 1in. Plane the fillets so that they taper slightly at the bottom then tap them into the gaps with a hammer and block of wood. Use a plane to shave the top edges of the fillets flush with the tops of the floorboards. Make sure the ends of fillets meet on a joist: secure them to the joists with brads.

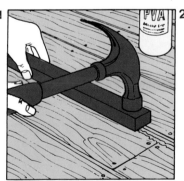
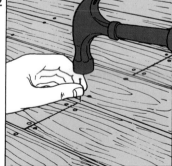

1 Filling the gap between square-edge floorboards with a glued wooden fillet hammered into position; use papier mâché for gaps below ¼in.
2 Fixing the fillet to the center of a joist with a 1½in panel pin; hammer gently and punch the head below the surface of the wood.
3 Planing the raised edge of the fillet flush with the boards using a smoothing-plane; allow the glue to set before planing.

If there are fairly wide gaps between all the boards, it may be more satisfactory to relay them closer together (see page 43), adding a narrow filler board at one side of the floor.

Damaged boards

Damaged sections of boards should be cut out and replaced, or a new board fitted if the damage is substantial. First check that there are no pipes or cables running below the damaged section, otherwise you will have to remove the entire board in case you cut into them by accident.

To cut out a section of board, first find the edges of the joists at each end. Do this by sliding a knife blade along the gap between the boards. If the boards are tongued-and-grooved, you will have to cut through the tongues by drilling a starting hole and using a keyhole saw or with a circular saw set to the depth of the board.

Drill a starting hole for the saw just in from the edge of each joist and cut through the board at each end in line with the joist edges.

Lift out the damaged section; if it is nailed to intermediate joists, lever it free using a masonry chisel and a stout length of wood. Lever the board upwards at the fixings with a chisel until you have lifted the end enough to be able to slide the wood below it, while resting it on the tops of the boards on each side. Pushing down on the end of the board will spring the fixings from the joist. Continue in this fashion until you have freed the board. A complete floorboard can be removed in the same way.

Screw or nail lengths of 2in sq batten to the sides of the joists flush with the undersides of the old boards. Then nail a new section of floorboard to the tops of the battens.

Sagging joists

On wide, unsupported spans, the joists may sag in the centre of the floor, giving it a slightly "dished" surface. To overcome this, add packing pieces to the tops of the affected joists.

Lift the floorboards and place a straightedge across the joists at several points. Measure any gap between the tops of the joints and the straightedge and use the measurements to mark out lengths of softwood batten. These must be the same width as the joists. Plane the battens to size and nail them to the tops of the affected joists. Finally, re-lay the floorboards.

RENEWING FLOOR JOISTS

You may find that a problem floor is simply due to one or two joists having become twisted and this can be cured by toe-nailing tight fitting wooden struts between them. However, if the wood is being eaten away by insects or rot, you will have no option but to replace every affected piece.

Removing the old joists

Lever up a sufficient number of floorboards to get at the affected joists, using a claw-headed hammer with a wooden batten to help leverage. Pull out all the nails and stack the boards so that you can replace them in the same order.

If only a small section of a joist is damaged, the affected area can easily be sawn out and replaced. However, for safety, make sure that the cuts are at least 24in beyond the damage.

Removal of a complete joist will mean levering it from its wall plates at each end, and also any intermediate wall plates. If the ends are set in sockets in the wall, cut through the joist just short of the wall and pull the stubs out. Brick up the sockets, cementing metal hangers into the top joints.

Fitting the new joist

If only a section of joist has been removed, cut a new piece of joist to the same size plus extra wood so that it will overlap the ends by at least 18in. Bolt this to the old joist with two carriage bolts at each end.

If a complete joist is to be fitted, trim back its ends to a taper so that there is no chance of it touching the external walls. Toe-nail the joist to its wall-plates.

If the wall plates themselves are affected, replace them at the same time, simply laying them on top of the sleeper walls. Make sure you prevent contact with the masonry by laying a strip of flexible flashing along the wall first. It is recommended that pressure treated lumber be used for replacement sections.

Something to watch out for are pipe and cable runs below the floor. Pipes are usually set in shallow-cut notches in the tops of the joists and cables pass through holes drilled in them.

Always remove the fuse, or flip the circuit breaker, controlling any underfloor electrical circuit before work begins. Cut the cable out of the old joist by making two saw cuts down to the hole. Make similar cuts in the new joist and glue the offcut back for added protection. Alternatively, disconnect the cable from the nearest fitting and thread it through the holes.

1 Sawing through a rotten floor joist to one side of the wall-plate; new joists overlap the existing one and are bolted to them.

2 With the wall-plate removed, renewing the flashing on sleeper wall; flashing should overlap both edges of wall.

3 Laying a new wall-plate on the flashing; take care that there is no dirt on the flashing so that the plate is supported along its length.

4 If the wall-plate is deeper than the original, you may need to notch the joists to maintain the old floor-level.

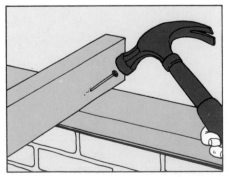

5 Fixing a joist to the wall-plate by toe-nailing; a heavy object held behind the joist to prevent it from moving.

6 Coating the end of a joist with liquid preservative.

•CHECKPOINT•

RELAYING FLOORBOARDS

Buy boards at least two weeks before starting work and stack them in the room in which they will be laid. This will allow them to dry out properly, preventing shrinkage later. Ideally, choose tongued-and-grooved boards (T&G), but if you are just replacing odd boards, square-edged ones would be better. In the latter case, make sure you get the right size: 4in and 6in are common widths and the usual finished thickness is ¾in, but thicker boards are available.

Removing the old boards

Lift the second board in from the wall, using the method described on page 41. Then use a length of stout wood to lever up the others. Take care along the walls, since the boards are likely to be tucked under the baseboard. Tidy up the joists by pulling out any remaining nails and fitting packing strips if necessary.

Fitting the boards

Fit four or five boards at a time, keeping any end joints between them to a minimum. Where joints cannot be avoided, make sure the boards meet at the center of a joist and that their ends are cut square. Use up offcuts when you can and stagger the end joints so they do not all fall in a line.

Mark and cut the first board to clear any obstructions and fit it up against the wall. Force a chisel blade into the top of the joists and use it to lever the board tight against the wall while you drive two nails through it into each joist. Use cut floor brads at least twice the length of the depth of the board.

If you are using T&G boards, the groove of this first board should face away from the wall and be nearer the joist than the top. Set the next four boards in place and push them tightly together using wooden wedges or floor cramps. In the former case, nail a length of wood temporarily across the joists and fit pairs of opposing wooden wedges between it and the boards. Tapping the wedges together will force the boards tight up against each other. Floor cramps clamp to the

joists and when tightened exert great force against the edges of the board, (you should be able to get them from a good tool rental company).

In both cases, cut short offcuts of floorboard to fit between the edges of the boards and the wedges or cramps to protect the board edges. With the boards cramped tight, nail the outermost one down. Then remove the wedges or cramps and nail the remainder.

Continue in this way across the room. Where there are pipes or cables below the floor that you might want to reach in the future, screw the boards down. Cut off the tongues of T&G boards to make lifting easy.

The final boards

Stop within the width of two boards from the far wall since you will not be able to cramp these last boards. To fit the final boards, first lay a full board up against the last one to be nailed down. Lever it tight up against this board with a chisel. Next, take a short offcut of floorboard and hold it against the base so that its other edge overlaps the full board. Hold a pencil against the edge of the offcut and run it along the full board to mark the profile of the wall on it.

Cut the board along the pencil line and then refit it, but this time along the wall, springing in a full board between it and the others at the same time. Nail both boards down.

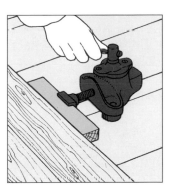

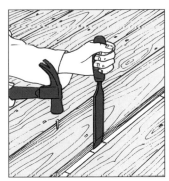

2 Compacting boards using a flooring clamp; position it on top of a joist and, with scrap wood as packing, force the boards together.

3 Levering boards together with an old chisel; hammer it vertically into the top of a joist and pull towards the board while nailing.

4 Fitting the last T & G boards: plane off two tongues, position one board against previous groove and scribe along second board.

5 After cutting the first board along the line and placing the cut board against the baseboard; pressing the two planed boards into position.

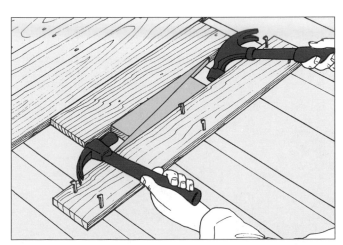

1 Using folding wedges to pack boards tightly; nail an offcut temporarily across the joists for the wedges to bear on and tap the ends inwards.

SOLID CONCRETE FLOORS

Solid concrete floors in modern houses are usually made up of a layer of gravel, topped by a layer of concrete (the subfloor), on top of which there is a waterproof membrane linked to the flashing in the base of the surrounding walls and finally a screed of mortar, which provides a smooth, level surface for your floorcovering. This type of construction is very tough, but even so, defects can occur; cracks, uneven surfaces and damp patches due to faulty waterproof membrane are all common problems.

Rotten wooden floors can be replaced with solid concrete ones relatively cheaply and they have the added advantage of providing a much more stable surface for laying something like quarry tiles or wood blocks. In this instance, however, you must incorporate pipework air ducts to link any ventilation holes or grilles in the external walls with the suspended wooden floors in adjacent rooms.

Uneven floors

If the surface of the floor is uneven you can smooth it with a self-leveling floor screed. Supplied in powder form for mixing with water or latex (depending on which it is based) the screed provides a smooth ⅛in layer on which you can lay floorcoverings.

Pour small amounts of screed onto the floor at a time and trowel roughly level. There is no need to work out trowel marks, since they gradually settle out. Before you apply the screed you must remove the baseboards and make sure there are no major cracks or depressions in the floor – fill these as previously described. Nail a batten temporarily across the threshold of any interconnecting doorway to provide a positive edge to the screed. When it has set, remove the batten and trowel a narrow sloping fillet of mortar along the edge to blend it into the adjoining floor.

Water-proof membranes may be thick plastic sheet, PVC, butyl rubber or painted-on bitumen emulsion, and to be effective they must provide a continuous layer across the floor and be joined to the wall flashing. If the waterproof membrane becomes punctured, damp patches will appear on the floorcovering. Small areas of damp can be treated by breaking through the surface screed and coating the damaged area of waterproof membrane with bitumen emulsion, then rescreeding with mortar.

If the problem is widespread, or if the floor has no waterproof membrane at all, the real solution is to dig it all up and lay a new floor.

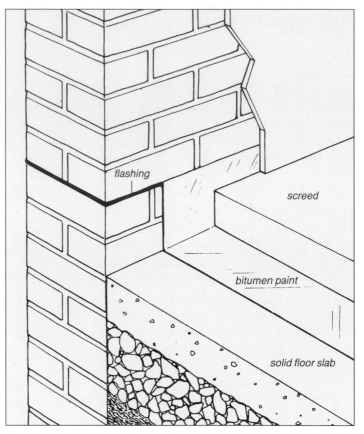

1 A solid floor painted with three coats of bitumen; this is taken up the wall to the flashing, and a 2in screed laid on top.

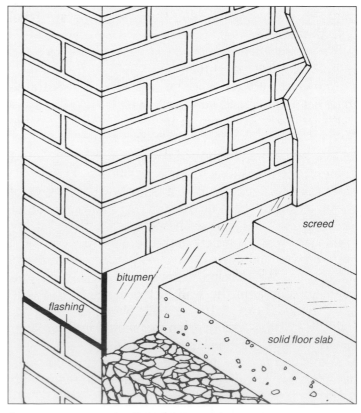

2 If the flashing is below floor-level, a groove must be cut and the bitumen emulsion taken down the groove to the flashing.

CASTING A SOLID FLOOR

The first job is to remove the old floor and dig out the ground below to at least 12in below the final floor level. Lever up an old wooden floor and saw through the joists for easy removal. Then demolish the dwarf walls. Break up a concrete floor: the best way is with a rented jack hammer. Keep the rubble for use as a bed for the concrete later. Wear stout boots, thick gloves, overalls and safety goggles.

Preparing the site
Find the flashing in the walls; it may be a layer of slate or bitumen, or one or two courses of engineering bricks. If necessary, chip away the plaster to find it.

If the floor in the next room is of suspended wood, lay plastic drain pipes between any airbricks and the inter-connecting door threshold, setting them in place with bits of stone or brick: this is vital to provide ventilation throughout the floor. Build a retaining wall across the threshold with concrete building blocks.

Next make up some datum pegs from 2 × 1in sawn softwood marked with the depths of the bed and concrete subfloor layers: 6in and 4in respectively. Cut a point on one end of the pegs then drive a peg into the ground near a given reference point, to indicate the surface of the floor. Drive the other pegs in at 3ft intervals, checking that their tops are level with the first.

Constructing the slab
Put down the brick and stone bed, leveling it with the marks on the pegs and compacting it well with a purpose-made tamper. Spread a layer of damp builder's sand over the top to fill any voids.

The concrete for the subfloor should be of 1 part cement: 2½ parts concreting sand: 4 parts gravel.

Lay the concrete so that it is level with the tops of the pegs, tamping it down well and drawing a stout batten across the tops of the pegs to level it. Fill any hollows with more concrete then tamp again.

When the concrete has cured, lay the cleavage membrane. With bitumen emulsion apply about three coats, taking it up the wall to the flashing. If plastic sheet is used, tack it to the walls above the flashing. Fold the corners and overlap the sheets by 8 to 12in, sealing the join with building adhesive.

Use 1 × 2in battens to divide the floor into 3ft wide bays for the finishing screed. Set them in place with dabs of mortar, level if necessary by packing offcuts underneath: check with a spirit level.

Fill the bays with a 3:1 mortar mix and draw it off

level with a straight-edged batten held across the tops of the dividing battens. When two bays have been completed, lift out the batten in between and fill the resulting slot with mortar. Then trowel both bays smooth with a metal trowel. When the mortar has stiffened, give it a final polish with a wetted trowel.

1 Level the second datum peg with the reference peg. Use a level on a straight-edge. Space pegs at 3ft intervals.

2 Binding the compacted gravel layer with damp builder's sand to fill any voids in the surface.

3 Laying concrete; spread it out evenly then compact and level with the peg tops using a stout beam. Work backwards to the door.

4 Tacking plastic waterproof membrane to the wall above the flashing; make neat folds at corners and overlap the sheets by about 12in.

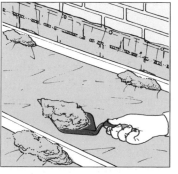

5 Dividing the floor into bays with 2 × 1in battens on edge, held with blobs of mortar; level with packing if necessary.

6 Leveling off the tamped mortar in the first bay by drawing a straight edge along the tops of the dividing battens.

REPAIRING AN OLD CEILING

There are two types of ceiling construction, depending on their age. Early ceilings were made by nailing thin strips of wood (laths) to the joists so that there were narrow gaps between them. Plaster, often reinforced with animal hair, was then spread over the laths and forced through the gaps in between. The ridges so formed are called "nibs" and these hold the ceiling together.

The more modern method of constructing a ceiling is to nail sheets of gypsumboard to the joists and cover them with a thin skim coat of plaster.

Dealing with cracks

Cracks are the most common form of damage found in a ceiling and if they are only fine they can be filled with a filler compound. However, if they are wide and cover a large area of the ceiling the structure will be dangerously weak and should be replaced.

If a plasterboard ceiling sags it is probably because the fixing nails have loosened. Refix the affected area by renailing with 2in drywall nails spaced 6in apart.

Patching damaged areas

If plaster has fallen away from the laths but they appear to be in good condition, replaster them after cutting back the original plaster to make a regular shape and reach sound plaster. Undercut the edges of the plaster and make sure there is no old plaster left between the laths. Then treat the area with an adhesive.

When plastering always work across the laths, spreading on a thin coat of bonding plaster first and keying it with a scratch comb made by knocking a row of nails into the edge of a short batten. Apply another coat of bonding plaster and key this with a devilling float, pressing it down to allow for two thin finishing coats. Polish these when hard with a wetted steel trowel.

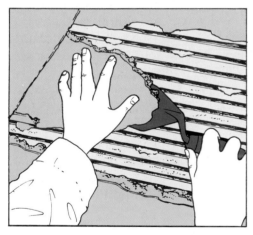

1 Levering off the damaged plaster from the laths with a trowel; clear the area within the marked lines and undercut the edges.

2 Applying a coat of bonding plaster across the laths after brushing on PVA adhesive; press plaster well into laths.

3 Keying the plaster with a scratch comb, working across the laths to avoid knocking out any plaster.

4 Applying a thicker second coat of bonding plaster over the first, taking it onto the edges of the original plaster.

5 Ruling off the second coat using a long aluminum float to flatten high spots and make low areas show up.

6 After keying the second coat, applying two thin coats of finishing plaster; give a final polish with a wetted metal trowel.

REMOVING AN OLD CEILING

Taking down an old lath-and-plaster ceiling is an extremely dirty and dusty job, so before you start you must take the necessary action to protect both yourself and the other rooms in the house.

Protective clothing is essential and you will need to wear overalls, safety goggles, a facemask and thick gloves. But the most important item is a construction worker's hard hat, which you can rent or buy. Hopefully the ceiling will come down under your control, but it is as well to be prepared for unexpected falls.

Because so much dust will be flying about, strip the room of all furnishings and seal the connecting doors to other rooms with plastic sheets or old blankets. It is a good idea to spread a large, thick plastic sheet across the floor to make collecting the debris easier, and you should have a good supply of thick plastic sacks to hand for bagging up the rubbish. If the ceiling is very large, it may be worthwhile renting a small container to dispose of the old ceiling.

Providing access
You need to be able to reach the ceiling easily so that you can lever sections of it away from the joists. For simplicity, place a scaffold board between two step ladders so that your head will be about 6in from the ceiling – a ladder on its own is not suitable. An alternative is to rent sections of scaffold tower to make small access platforms, but this is probably only worthwhile if the job is large.

Any ceiling-mounted lighting fittings must be removed (after turning off the power at the service panel or removing the appropriate fuse). Pull the supply cable back above the ceiling if you can get to it; if not tape up the ends and leave it hanging.

If the ceiling is immediately below the roof space, check that there are no other electricity cables lying across the top of the ceiling which you may snag as you remove it. Clip these to the joists.

Any dirt and dust above the ceiling should be removed with a vacuum cleaner.

Many attics are insulated with various materials laid across the top of the ceiling and obviously, these must be removed. Roll up glass fiber mat insulation and put into plastic garbage bags stacked in an unaffected part of the attic until it can be replaced. Loose-fill insulation should be scooped up and poured into garbage bags; or suck it up with an industrial vacuum cleaner before bagging it.

Removing the ceiling
You can use a large claw hammer or a flat chisel and hammer to remove the old ceiling, although you might find the former easier as the latter will mean holding both arms above your head, which can be very tiring.

Hack into the plaster, levering pieces away until you have exposed a large area of laths. Prise these from the joists, always working away from yourself so that any falls will not be on top of you.

Continue working across the room until the entire ceiling is removed. Using pincers, pull out all the lath-fixing nails from the joists. Work round the edges of the ceiling with a chisel to clean up the plaster on the walls.

1 Prising away laths from the joists using a claw hammer, after levering off a section of plaster; work away from you for safety.

2 Removing the lath-fixing nails with a pair of pincers; make sure none remain so that the new ceiling will fit tight against the joists.

FITTING A NEW CEILING

Gypsumboard for ceilings comes in two thicknesses: ⅜in and ½in, the former being suitable for use where the joist spacing is no more than 18in and the latter where the joists are up to 2ft apart. The standard sheet sizes are 8 and 10 × 4ft. You may find the smaller sheets easier to handle and you can cut them in half to make them even more manageable. The edges should meet on the joist centerlines, so you will probably have to trim them slightly anyway.

Preparing the joists

The first job is to nail lengths of 2in sq or 2 x 3in wood along the walls parallel with the joists so that its lower edge is level with the undersides of the joists. Then fit more short lengths of wood to the walls between the ends of the joists to provide support for the edges of the boards.

The sheets of gypsumboard must be fitted with their long edges at right-angles to the joists. Toe-nail more lengths of batten to act as bracing between the joists so that the inner edges of the sheets will fall on their center lines. A length of batten marked with the board width will help position them accurately.

Finally, mark the position of each joist on the walls as a guide for nailing the sheets in place.

Trimming the sheets

To cut sheets to size, use a utility knife and steel straightedge. Cut down through one face of the board, snap back the waste against a batten and run the knife blade down the crease from the other side.

Fitting the gypsumboard

If you intend plastering the ceiling, fit the gypsumboard gray side down. For painting or papering directly over the top, leave the ivory side showing.

Holding large sheets of board against the ceiling for nailing can be difficult so nail lengths of 2 × 1in batten together to form T-shaped props with which a helper can support it while being nailed in place.

Nail the first board in place, working from the center outwards and spacing the nails at 6in intervals. Drive them home so that they just dimple the surface; to be filled later. Use 1¼in gypsumboard nails for thinner sheets and 1½in for thicker kinds.

Continue in this way, working across the ceiling. Keep any cut edges up against the wall, but if this is not possible make sure they meet on a joist with a slight gap in between for filling; stagger the joints.

When you have clad the entire ceiling, seal the joints between the sheets and, if you prefer, apply a thin skim coat of plaster (see opposite).

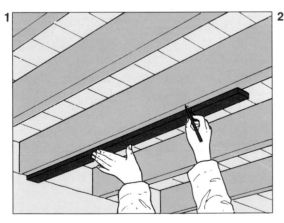

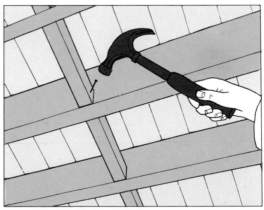

1 Marking the center line for the bracing on the joists using a batten marked with the width of a board as a guide.
2 Toe-nailing the bracing in line between the joists; cut it to a tight fit and tap them in flush with the joists.

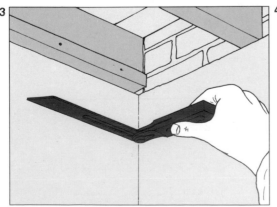

3 Using a sliding bevel to transfer the angle between walls to the gypsumboard; continue the line across with a straight-edge.
4 Propping the gypsumboard while nailing it; the edges of the board should be on the center lines of the joists and bracing.

FINISHING PLASTERBOARD

Finishing an Imperial ceiling with a coat of plaster is carried out in a similar manner to finishing off a drywall partition (see pages 18 to 27). However, when working above your head (which often presents difficulties of its own) it is best to apply small amounts of plaster at a time to avoid tiring your arms.

Deal with the joints first, spreading a thin layer of plaster down the center of each one and pressing lengths of 2in wide nylon mesh or paper tape into the wet plaster with your trowel. Lightly trowel over the tape then apply another thin layer of plaster on top.

Divide into handy bays; fill in each bay with a thin layer of plaster, but not over the joints. Hold the trowel blade at 30° to the surface of the ceiling; the back edge about 1/16in clear of the board to provide an even layer. Reduce the blade angle as the plaster spreads and pinch the back edge in as you complete the stroke to stop the plaster falling off. Work away from you to avoid flicking plaster into your face.

When you have filled in all the bays, go over the

1 Bedding jointing tape into wet plaster over the joint between two sheets; press it into one end of the joint with the trowel and feed it along.

2 Applying a thin layer of plaster between the taped joints; hold the trowel at 30° to the surface, gradually reducing the angle.

3 Ruling off with a long aluminum float after applying a second layer of plaster over the entire area; work outwards from one of the wall angles.

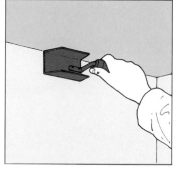

4 Finishing off the angle between wall and ceiling with an internal-angle trowel to leave a gently curved join.

entire ceiling with another thin layer of plaster. Rule it off with a long metal straightedge to remove the high patches and show up the low spots, which should be filled with a thin coat of plaster.

How you treat the angle between the ceiling and walls depends on whether you are replastering the walls at the same time or not. If not, simply run the corner of the trowel blade along the angle from the ceiling and wall sides to cut out the angle neatly. If you are replastering the wall as well, lay on the floating coat then tape the joint between the wall and ceiling before applying the finish coats. Finish the corner as normal (see page 24).

Finally, polish the hardened plaster with a clean, wetted trowel blade.

Filling the joints

If you intend papering or painting directly over the drywall, the joints must first be made to "disappear". For this you will need drywall joint compound, paper jointing tape and joint finish (see below).

First spread a layer of compound down the seam and, with a taping knife, press the tape into it. Apply another layer of compound over the top, feathering the edges by going over them with a damp sponge.

When the compound has dried, apply a finishing layer, feathering its edges in the same way. Treat the nail head depressions with compound and finish in the same manner.

At the angles between wall and cciling, fill large gaps with compound; then apply compound to both wall and ceiling and press a creased length of tape into it. Apply two more layers of compound to wall and ceiling, feathering the edges of each one.

Bedding paper jointing tape into joint compound; cover with more compound, feather the edges and, after it dries, apply another coat.

Applying a layer of joint finish compound over the folded paper jointing tape at the wall angle; joint finish compound is used at all stages.

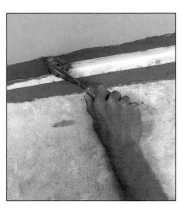

STAIRCASES

Staircases are often taken for granted yet they are complex pieces of carpentry which give many years of trouble-free use. They rarely need replacing: just as well, since they are often tailor-made to fit. Even so you can buy ready made versions, which cater for common storey heights and these can often be easily adapted to fit exactly.

Staircase construction

A staircase comprises a number of steps fixed between two long boards which are fixed to the joists of the floors they connect. These boards are called strings, the horizontal surfaces of the steps are called treads and sometimes they have vertical boards between them known as risers.

Strings can be in two forms: closed and cut. With the former the ends of the treads and risers are housed in shallow slots cut in the face of the string and held there by wedges driven in from behind and below. The risers are fixed to the treads below with housing joints or screws, and to the treads above by triangular blocks glued and nailed in place. The top edge of a cut string is shaped to provide horizontal ledges to which the treads are fixed. Sometimes both forms of string will be used in the same staircase, the closed string being fixed against a wall with the cut string on the outside.

Further support for the steps can be provided by a beam that runs below the treads and risers parallel to the strings. This is known as a carriage.

There are two basic types of staircase: the closed tread and open tread. Of the two, the former is most common, having treads and risers in a boxed-in construction. The underside of the strings are usually clad with lath and plaster or gypsumboard or there may be a closet below the stairs. The latter is preferable since it allows easy inspection and repair. The open tread staircase has no risers and is completely exposed.

In a closed tread staircase the treads are about 1in thick and will overhang the risers by a similar amount, their leading edges or noses being rounded off. A decorative molding is often fitted below the nose. An open tread staircase will tend to have thicker treads because they are not supported by risers, although sometimes a batten will be set on edge immediately below them to stiffen the tread.

All staircases must have at least one handrail and if wide they must have one on each side, depending on the requirements of your local code. The handrail forms part of the balustrade, the other parts of which are the newel posts and balusters.

The newel posts fit at each end of the stairs with the handrail running between them. Not only do they support the handrail but often the strings as well which will be slotted into them and fixed with wooden dowels. Further support for the handrail is provided by the balusters which fit between it and the strings.

Staircase styles

Though straight staircases are common, where space is limited it is often necessary for the stairs to change direction on the way up. A small quarter landing is used to provide a 90° change of direction and a half landing will turn the stairs back on themselves.

If there is not room for a half or quarter landing a turn can be put into the stairs by inserting triangular treads called winders. Winders are also used in spiral staircases which can be great space savers. Unfortunately they are not very practical since carrying furniture and other bulky items up them is difficult.

An additional handrail attached to the wall ensures safe ascent or descent for the left- or right-handed on wide stairs.

REPAIRS TO TREADS

Actual physical damage to stair treads is rare and will probably be limited purely to split or broken nosings. These can be repaired by cutting them off flush with the riser below, using a chisel, and pinning on a new molding.

A much more common problem, particularly in older houses, is creaking as a result of the treads becoming loose. The ease with which this can be fixed depends very much on whether you can get to the underside of the stairs or not. If you can, simply pin and glue 2 x 2in triangular blocks of wood between the treads and risers below, and drive screws up through the tread into the riser above. This is the only way you can fix a staircase with closed strings.

Cut strings

If the staircase has one or two cut strings, you can make the repair from above. First prise off the molding from below the tread nose and the molding holding the foot of the baluster in place, using an old chisel. Run a hacksaw blade along the gap between the back of the tread and upper riser, cutting through any fixings. Alternatively, cut through the riser itself with a backsaw. Drive a chisel blade between the tread nose and riser and lever it free. Then you can remove the risers if damaged.

If necessary, cut a new tread and riser from wood of the same size as the originals.

Closed strings

If one of the strings is closed, glue and pin supporting blocks to it for the ends of the riser and tread. Use offcuts of the tread and riser wood as positioning guides to ensure a tight fit. Then glue and pin the riser in place.

Pin and glue more blocks to the top of the lower riser and then glue the tread on top, strengthening the bond by driving screws or nails down through the ends into the cut string or strings. Do not drive any screws or nails through the leading edge of the tread as they may become exposed as the tread wears.

Refit the baluster, pinning it to the handrail and then pin the retaining molding to the end of the tread. Finally, refit the molding beneath the tread nose.

If you can reach the underside of a closed string staircase, you can replace treads or risers by removing their retaining wedges with a chisel and sliding the damaged parts out. Slot the new pieces in and fit new wedges. If a carriage runs down the centre of the stairs, however, the work is best left to a joiner or builder.

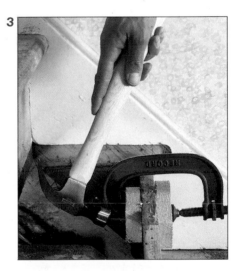

1 Replacing a tread: prising off the planted molding with an old chisel and mallet to free the balusters.
2 Prising up the open end of the tread from the string; remove the tread by wiggling it free from the closed string.
3 Nailing and gluing a reinforcing block to the riser below; also nail a batten below the groove in the closed string.
4 Shaping the nosing of the new tread with a spokeshave; keep the curve uniform and ensure that the front edge is straight.
5 After applying adhesive to the edges of the risers and battens; screwing the new tread to the batten on the closed string.

BANISTERS

Of all the sections of the staircase likely to suffer damage, the handrails come top of the list. Yet they play an important safety role by preventing people from falling down the stairs and so must be kept in good repair.

The balusters are the most vulnerable part of the assembly and may become loose or broken.

A loose toe-nailed baluster can be tapped free with a mallet and block of wood, the nails removed and the holes opened out with a drill to accept countersunk screws. Then glue and screw it in place.

If the ends of the baluster are held by mortise joints, you can stop the baluster rattling about by driving narrow wedges into the gaps around the ends, having first smeared them with glue. Cut the ends of the wedges flush with the surface of the string or handrail as appropriate. Sometimes, the balusters are held by thin strips of wood nailed in place between the ends of adjacent balusters. In this case, carefully prise off the strips on each side of the loose baluster and replace them with slightly longer ones.

If the baluster is actually broken, you can either replace it with a new one (assuming you can get one to match) or glue it back together, reinforcing the joint with dowels or screws. Toe-nailed balusters are easily removed as described above, as are those held by nailed-on capping pieces. However, if they are mortised into the string and handrail, you may have to saw through the ends to remove the baluster. Then glue blocks of wood into the mortise, plane them flush, cut the new baluster to fit and glue and screw it in place as you would a skewnailed version.

If a section of handrail is broken, you can make a simple repair by screwing a metal plate underneath across the break. Alternatively, you can cut out a section and fit a new piece, using special handrail bolts or screws. These need matching holes in the ends of the old and new rail, and the easiest way of marking them is with a paper template that matches the profile of the rail with the hole center marked on it. Hold the template over the end of each piece and mark the hole center by punching through with a nail. Additional holes must be drilled or cut with a chisel into the underside of the rail so that the nuts securing the bolt can be tightened.

Newel posts are unlikely to break, but if they do, they must be replaced completely. To remove it, you will have to lift the adjacent floorboards and unbolt the base from the joists. Then drive out the dowels holding the handrail and string to it. Finally, tap the newel post free – it may help to cut it into sections with a saw.

Use the old post as a guide for marking out the new one, making sure the mortises and dowel holes are all positioned correctly. Treat the base of the post with preservative and refit it, gluing the string and handrail in place and reinforcing the joints with fresh dowels.

Staircase kits
Whether you are installing a new staircase or simply repairing an existing one, the range of components available in kit form makes the task much easier.

The stairs may be ready-assembled and consist of 12 or 14 treads for a full flight or six treads for a half-flight; they are available with or without risers (for closed or open tread styles) and bullnose steps allow extra versatility at floor-level.

The newels, baluster spindles, rails and fittings are manufactured in a wide variety of styles, from traditional to contemporary. The timber, which includes mahogany and hemlock, is usually sanded ready for varnishing or staining.

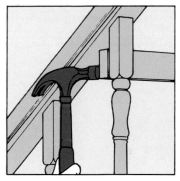
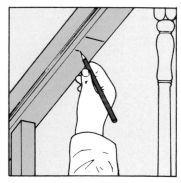

1 Removing a loose baluster by tapping it away from the handrail; use a hammer or mallet wood with a block to protect the wood.

2 Marking the position for refixing the baluster on the underside of the handrail; drill and countersink the baluster before fixing.

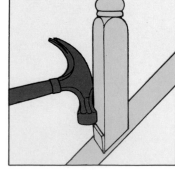

3 Screwing the baluster back to the handrail; clamp a stop to the handrail to prevent the baluster from sliding out of position.

4 Wedging the bottom of a baluster into its notch; tap a wedge between the baluster and the string after applying woodworking adhesive.

CHAPTER 3

ROOFS

In the same way that floors and ceilings are inevitably affected by remodeling the interior of the house, so too is the roof — particularly when dormer windows are installed or a room extension is built on. And after making such changes to your living space, you may wish to replace missing or broken roof slates or tiles, repoint the eaves or repair the verges, valleys and hips. This chapter shows all the professional techniques and skills required for making these improvements and repairs, while at the same time, making sure that the roof over your head is thoroughly safe and weatherproof.

•CHECKPOINT•

ACCESS TO THE ROOF

Because roofs are so far from the ground you must make sure that you have both a safe means of reaching the roof and a safe working platform once you get there. You can reach the roof by a normal extending ladder, but you must take steps to prevent it toppling over. Always set the feet so that they are about a quarter of the ladder's length away from the wall against which it is leaning. On concrete you can prevent the feet from slipping by standing them on a piece of sacking. On soft ground, set them on a board with a batten nailed on the edge as a stop. Drive stakes into the ground to stop the board moving. You can also tie the feet of the ladder to stakes driven into the ground.

Tie the top of the ladder to a screw-eye fixed to the fascia board or even to a batten spanning the inside of a window opening, and make sure it extends beyond the eaves by at least 3ft. Do not rest it on the guttering, which could break under the weight; rent a ladder stay to hold it away from the gutter, propped against the wall below the fascia.

If the work you are doing means carrying up bulky materials, you would be better off renting a staging tower which will provide a platform at roof level for stacking materials. These are sectional in construction and often have wheels at the bottom for maneuvering them into position.

If you use a staging tower always make sure it is set on firm, level ground (with boards under the feet if necessary), that any wheels are locked up and that it is fitted with outriggers or tied to the building to stop it toppling. Construct a

platform at the top from stout boards, making sure there are toe boards round the edges and a handrail. Always climb up inside the tower and not on the outside, and do not lean ladders against the tower.

Traversing the roof

Roof tiles and slates are easily broken, so you must have some means of spreading your weight as you climb across them. The best way is with a roof or "cat" ladder. This has a large hook, which locates over the ridge of the roof, and usually a pair of small wheels. The wheels allow you to run the ladder up the roof before turning it over to engage the hook over the ridge of the roof.

While you can do many jobs working from a roof ladder, for any major work on a chimney, it is better to build a staging tower around it, supporting the feet on boards to spread the weight.

1 Tying the bottom of a ladder to pegs driven into the ground; rest the base on a thick board with a batten nailed to it.

2 Using a ladder stay to support the top of the ladder away from the guttering; it is tied to a batten inside the window.

3 Locking the wheels of a staging tower by depressing the handle; the wheels must rest on strong level boards.

4 At the top of the staging tower, slotting in the toe-board round the boarded platform.

5 Pushing a roof-ladder up to the ridge on the wheels attached to it; the wheels prevent damage to the roof covering.

6 When the end of the roof-ladder is over the ridge; turning it over to hook on the ridge, leaving the rungs uppermost.

REPLACING SINGLE TILES/SLATES

Tiles

Because the tile you want to replace will be hooked over the batten, you need some means of lifting the adjacent tiles sufficiently to be able to lift the broken one from the batten. The best method is with wooden wedges which you can cut from lengths of 2 × 1in batten, about 6in long. You will need two of these and more if the tiles are of the interlocking type.

Push the wedges beneath the tiles of the course above the broken one so there is a big enough gap for the nibs (lugs along the top edge edge of the tile) to clear the batten. Lift the tile up and remove it. If you can not get hold of it because the end has broken off, slide the blade of a bricklayer's trowel underneath the remaining portion and use this to lift it clear.

If it is nailed in place, try wiggling it from side to side, which may pull the nails free. If not, you will have to cut through the nails with a slate ripper (see pages 56–57), a pair of pincers or a hacksaw blade.

If the tile is of the interlocking type, you will have to wedge up one of its neighbours to free it.

Fit the replacement tile by lifting it into place with the trowel blade, hooking the nibs over the batten – without nailing; the tiles above will hold it fast.

Remove the wedges carefully to lower the surrounding tiles, making sure any interlocking ridges are properly engaged and that all tiles are sitting flat.

Slates

To remove a broken slate you will need a tool called a slate ripper. This has a thin, barbed blade for cutting through the two fixing nails, which are hidden by the slates above. Slide the ripper up under the broken slate, feeling for the nails. Hook the blade over one and tug downwards sharply to slice through it. Repeat for the second nail and slide the slate out.

If you have to cut the slate to size, scribe the size on its face and set it over the edge of a wooden batten; cut along the line with the heel of a trowel.

The new slate cannot be nailed in place because of the slates above. Instead, it is retained by a lead strip measuring 9 × 1in. Nail this to the batten (visible below the two exposed slates) with a galvanized nail.

Carefully lift the slates above and slide the new one into place so that the beveled edge along the bottom is uppermost. Bend up the end of the lead strip to retain it then make a second bend for extra strength.

Slates at the gable end of a roof will need a horizontal clip to stop them from sliding off the edge.

1 Raising the tiles above a broken one by sliding wooden wedges under the bottom edges; an adjacent tile must also be raised if interlocking.

2 Prising out the remains of the broken tile using the point of a bricklayer's trowel to lift the nibs over the batten.

3 If the tile was nailed to the batten; cutting through the fixing nails with a hacksaw blade held in a padsaw handle.

4 Sliding the replacement tile into position; use the trowel blade again to lift the nibs over the batten without nailing.

1 Sliding the clawed end of a slate-ripper under a damaged slate; hook the blade round the fixing nails and pull to cut them.

2 After removing the damaged slate; nailing a strip of lead to the exposed batten with a galvanized clout nail.

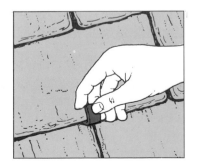

3 After sliding a new slate into the gap; bending up the strip of lead over the bottom edge to hold the slate in position.

•CHECKPOINT•

ATTIC ACCESS

Being able to get into the roof space of your home is important, not just because of the extra storage capacity it offers but also to be able to deal with emergencies like leaking roofs and burst pipes, and also to be able to install extra light fittings to the rooms below.

Most houses already have some form of hatchway providing access to the attic but it may not always be in the most convenient place, and in some instances there may be no access to the attic at all. In both situations you can make a new opening with comparatively little trouble.

The usual position of an attic hatchway is in a hall or over a landing, but in the latter case make sure it is not over the staircase itself. Do not put it near an external wall either if this meets the eaves of the roof, as there will not be enough headroom above the opening.

Another important consideration when positioning an opening is the space needed in the roof and in the room below for any attic ladder you intend fitting.

Having decided on the approximate position, locate the adjacent joists by tapping the ceiling and probing with a bradawl, or mark through from the loft if you can reach it by some other route.

Break through the ceiling between a pair of joists and open up the hole until you can make a saw cut alongside one of them. Then mark out the opening on the ceiling from this baseline. Its size will be determined by the joist spacing and since this will be too close to make the opening between the pair, it will have to span three. This means cutting through the center joist and linking it to the joists on each side with short "trimmer" joists. The wood used must be the same size as that of the original joists.

Before you cut through the intermediate joists, support the ceiling on each side of the opening with stout planks and wood or adjustable metal props (see page 27).

Line the opening with 1in thick planed wood the same depth as the joists and nailed in place flush with the ceiling. The corners of this can be simply butted together.

Then make up a plywood trapdoor for the opening, hinging it to the bottom of the lining and either fitting a magnetic catch on the opposite side or an automatic catch such as that supplied with an attic ladder.

Finally, nail lengths of mitered molding around the opening, driving the nails into the joists so that the molding holds the edges of the ceiling firmly in place.

1 Cutting along a joist with a keyhole saw to form the opening; continue with a panel saw. First, locate the joists with a bradawl.

2 After cutting out the opening, propping beneath the joist which is to be cut, using a strong length of wood.

3 Cutting through the joist, the thickness of the trimmer back from the opening; you will need a short panel saw for this job.

4 Nailing the trimmer joist to the end of the cut joist; nail through the outer joists into the ends of the trimmer.

5 Nailing the wood lining to the joists with oval nails; the bottom edge should be flush with the ceiling.

6 After fixing architrave around the opening; screwing the hinged trap-door to the lining.

FITTING AN ATTIC LADDER

When you want to get into your attic there is no reason why you should not use an ordinary ladder, provided it is secured to the opening in some way – by hooks and eyes perhaps, but whatever you do, never use a pair of step ladders. In trying to climb out of the attic and groping for the top of the steps with your foot, you could easily knock them over, leaving you stranded, or worse you might fall with the ladder causing physical injury.

One drawback to using a normal ladder is that you will need somewhere to store it and you will have to go to the trouble of digging it out of storage every time you want to get into the roof space — or it may be in use elsewhere in the house.

A much more satisfactory solution to the problem of climbing into your attic is the proprietary extendable attic ladder. This sits just above the trapdoor on hinges or pivots screwed to the inside or top of the opening frame and can be pulled down whenever you need it. Such a ladder, with its own built-in storage, makes your attic much more usable and accessible.

Types of ladder

Purpose-made attic ladders are usually produced in aluminum with 2 or 3in wide treads. Most have two or three sliding sections with a safety catch that must be released before they can be extended. Some are linked to the trapdoor by a special bracket so that they come immediately to hand when you open it up.

When closed, the ladder lies across the tops of the joists next to the trapdoor, but it swings upwards over the opening before it can be pulled down, so it is essential that there is enough height above the opening for this.

Another important factor is the size of the opening itself which must be large enough to allow the ladder to pass through. This is not usually a problem if you are making a new opening, but if you want to fit the ladder to an existing opening, you will have to take some careful measurements. You will also need to know the distance from the floor of the attic (not the ceiling) to the floor of the room below.

For extremely limited attic space, there is a concertina attic ladder that folds up compactly rather than sliding.

Attic ladders can be simple or complex in design with risers and balustrades just like a proper staircase. Most come with some form of automatic trapdoor catch operated by relatively light finger-tip pressure on the door itself.

Installing an attic ladder

Obviously, the method of installing an attic ladder varies from one make and model to another, but usually it is quite a simple procedure. Often all that is necessary is to screw the hinges or pivots to the framework of the opening (on the same side as the trapdoor hinges) and fit the automatic catch to the other side of the opening. There may also be travel stops to adjust on the ladder and a bracket to fit to the trapdoor to hold the ladder so that it is easily reached.

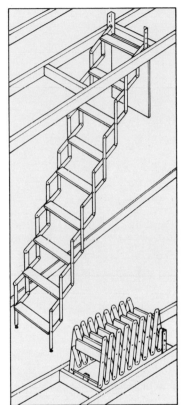

The supporting cradle for a sliding attic ladder hooks over the trimmer joist at the hinge end of the access door and is screwed in place.

A concertina attic ladder in the extended and stowed positions.

FITTING A DORMER WINDOW

In converting an attic the installation of one or more dormer windows will not only provide essential natural light but also increase the headroom over areas of floor that were previously unusable.

In addition to providing windows and extra floor space, with a dormer built up from eaves level, you can site a staircase immediately below it fixed to the external wall of the house, whereas normally it would have to run through the center for there to be enough headroom at the top.

Supporting the structure

Since several rafters will have to be cut through to

make the dormer, the framework must be strong enough to support the load previously borne by the cut rafters. It must also have support at floor level unless it is possible to set the framing directly on top of a loadbearing wall. The original attic joists would certainly not be strong enough. However, since a dormer will be put in as part of an attic conversion (see page 62) this is not really a problem. A strengthening framework and extra joists will have to be put in for the new attic floor and this can be made to support the dormer framework as well. This new framework is built directly onto the house load-bearing walls and is completely independent of the original attic joists and ceiling below.

Calculating the loads involved and designing the supporting framework is specialist work for an architect, engineer or a contractor.

Building the framework

The construction of the dormer framework would follow on from constructing the floor support structure. Once the dormer is complete, do the rest of the conversion work. Access to the roof will be needed so that bulky materials can be passed through from the outside after removing a few tiles or slates and cutting an opening in the roofing felt. An access tower and roof ladder are essential.

The first job is to build the framework of the dormer, making sure it is secure before cutting through the original rafters and removing them.

The first sections of framework to be erected are the two corner posts for the outer end of the dormer. There is no need to strip off all the roofing within the dormer area for this initial construction work; remove

only small sections of tiles and pass the framework through. In this way the roof can be kept reasonably weathertight for most of the time.

The corner posts stand on the supporting floor joists below and are linked immediately below rafter level by a horizontal beam. Short wooden studs are nailed between the purlin and the supporting floor beam. The purlin has two purposes: to tie the bottoms of the corner posts together and to support the lower ends of the original rafters when they are cut through. All the construction is toe-nailed to fit.

Next, nail a horizontal beam across the tops of the corner posts. The joists for the top of the dormer can then be fitted: nail their outer ends to the top of the header and pass them right through the roof and bolt them to the rafters on each side for stability.

If the roof of the dormer is to be flat, tapered wooden slats, called furring pieces, are nailed to the tops of the joists so that the roof will have a fall to the front for drainage. If the dormer is to have a pitched roof, a ridge board and additional rafters are installed above the joists.

Before removing the roof from within the dormer framework, fit additional trimmer rafters between the corner posts and the roof ridge bar (or hip rafter if the dormer is a wide one on a hipped roof). Cut shallow notches in the sides of the corner posts to take the ends of these trimmers, and nail in place.

To complete the framework, the roofing must be stripped off. Lift the tiles or slates (see page 57) from the battens, cut out the felt and saw through the battens to expose the joists: cut these off flush with the undersides of the dormer joists and level with the inner face of the new supporting purlin.

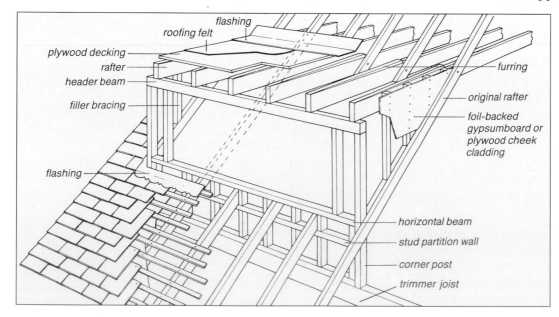

The framework structure of a dormer; apart from being rigid itself, it must also support the roof above and below. The corner posts are supported on an original trimmer joist, and the rafters rest on a header beam and are bolted to the rafters. A stud framework in the cheeks and front wall is clad with foil-backed drywall or plywood, and the roof is decked with plywood set to a fall with furrings. The window is fitted between filler bracing set between the corner posts and is supported on a horizontal beam.

Nail vertical studs between the trimmer rafters and the joists above to provide support for the side "cheek" cladding of the dormer, spacing them to take account of the width of the cladding sheets so that their edges always fall on the centerline of a stud.

Complete the framework by adding a wooden subframe to support the window itself. This is usually a horizontal beam set between the corner posts and supported below by short studs nailed to the top of the new purlin, and possibly to the sides of the cut rafters as well. The window will be narrower than the distance between the corner posts, so nail additional studs between the horizontal beam and header to support it at the sides.

Cladding the framework

The roof is covered first and if it is flat, it is decked with exterior grade plywood, butting the sheets together and nailing them to the supporting joists. To provide support for the flashing, slip a narrow strip of board under the roof at the junction with the dormer and nail it to the original rafters. To provide a certain degree of protection until the job is completed, you can add the first two layers of felt at this stage, taking them up under the original roof and leaving overlaps at the sides and front for finishing off.

Next the sides and front of the framework on either side of the window opening can be paneled in: you can use foil-backed gypsumboard for the cheeks. Nail it to the outside of the framework with the foil side outermost to prevent moisture penetration.

Fit lead soakers beneath the tiles on each side of the dormer; it may actually be easier to do this before cladding the sides, since they will slip in from the ends of the courses without the removal of the tiles.

Before finishing off cladding the sides, add flashing to the front of the dormer below the window opening, taking it over the top of the frame-supporting beam and down over the roof tiles or slates below.

If tiles are to be used for cladding, nail narrow battens horizontally around the dormer (the spacing being dictated by the tile size). If boarding is used, nail the battens on vertically. Overlapping tiles and boards are nailed on in pattern to keep out rainwater.

Fit window frames made from seasoned wood. A gutter is fixed along the front fascia board with a short down-pipe at one end which can be led down the corner of the dormer to discharge its contents over the roof below.

Finishing off inside

Having clad the outside of the dormer and glazed the window, finish off inside – this can be done at the same time as building the interior of the attic room.

While the framework is still exposed, however, glass fiber or polystyrene insulation can be fixed between the various frame members at the sides and in the roof before they are clad with drywall or whatever internal wall cladding is being used.

1 Passing the dormer rafters into the roof-space; they rest on the header and are attached to the rafters at the front and back of the roof.

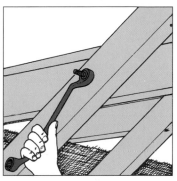

2 Bolting the dormer rafters to the main roof rafters; use hexagon-headed bolts and place a washer between the nut and the wood.

3 Tapping vertical bracing into place between the front purlin and the horizontal beam which will support the window frame.

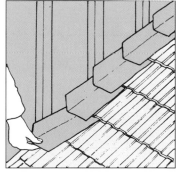

4 Sliding metal flashing under tiles adjacent to the dormer cheeks to form a drainage channel; the short side of the flashing is vertical.

5 Nailing foil-backed waterproof drywall to the cheeks after cutting to shape; slide it down inside the flashing and nail through into the noggings.

6 Screwing the window frame to the filler noggins after leveling it and checking that the diagonals are equal to ensure that it is square.

CONVERTING AN ATTIC

There are many points to consider before you can safely go ahead and convert your attic to living space. The first thing to do is to check the inside and the floor below to get some idea as to whether a conversion is possible or not.

The method of construction of the roof can present its own problems and some types do not lend themselves to conversion at all. Really heavy vertical posts supporting the ridge, with heavy cross-pieces below and diagonal struts, cannot be removed and they may be spaced too closely to allow rooms in between. Some modern houses have roofs made of prefabricated lightweight trussed rafters with no ridge bar at all, and these cannot be altered either.

How much space is available?

In assessing space the problems arise because what you will be trying to do is to create a roughly rectangular shape within a triangular one. An attic has a vast floor area – equal to the area of the floor below – but because the roof slopes inwards the amount of floor area which is of any real use can be quite small.

The design of the roof also has an effect on the

space available without making structural modifications to it. For a roof of any given size, a gable-ended design will have more immediately usable space than one with a gable at one end and a hip at the other. A roof with both ends hipped will offer even less room. This situation can be considerably improved by the addition of dormers but you need to decide whether the work involved will be worthwhile.

The pitch of the roof also has an effect; a low shallow pitched roof offers less space than a tall steeply-pitched one because of the need for a reasonable headroom over most of the floor. The Building Code usually stipulates a minimum headroom, but this only applies to a percentage of the floor area, so the rest of the floor area can have a lower headroom. This allows you to push the outer walls of the rooms out into the eaves to increase the size.

How will you reach the attic rooms?

Having the space available either as the roof stands or with the addition of dormers is one thing, but you must fit a proper staircase to the attic — so work out roughly where you could install it.

Ideally, the new flight of stairs should be fitted over the existing stairwell, but to do this you may have to break through the wall of an adjoining room with a consequent loss of space in that room. In this situation you would want to be sure that the space lost at the foot of the stairs would be regained together with a lot more space in the attic.

You should also take into account where the staircase will break through the ceiling into the attic. It will need quite a large opening and should not interfere with essential roof supports, chimneys, cisterns and pipework. You must have ample headroom at the base of the stairs, on the stairs and at the top of the stairs, although the latter can often be

Some of the original wooden members have been retained in this attic room to provide an open-plan division with no loss of light or space, and to break up the expanse of wood cladding on the ceilings and walls.

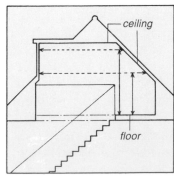

Usable floor area occurs where the headroom is at least 7'–0"; always check with your local Building Code.

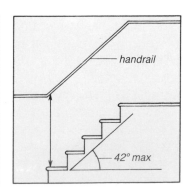

A new staircase should have: a maximum pitch of 38°, minimum headroom of 6ft 11in and a handrail 34in high. Check with your local Building Code.

provided by building out a dormer to the eaves.

If the house is a two storey building, the conversion of the attic will make it three storeys high and here you may run into another snag, with your local building code. The door that opens to the stairwell of a three-storey building may have to be self-closing and the walls, floors and door frames may need to offer half-to one-hour fire resistance. Often the floors and walls will be built to this standard anyway, but there are still the doors to be taken care of. Local Codes vary so always check with your local Building Codes before planning any building project.

Other considerations

There are other things to think about as well, such as what type of windows you will fit and where you will fit them. How will you supply electric light and power, heating and a water supply (if one of the rooms is to be a bathroom or powder room)?

Your lighting and power accessories will almost certainly need new circuits, which means having sufficient spare fuseways or breakers at the electric panel, or extending the existing service panel. If you intend extending your central heating system, check that the boiler has the extra capacity.

In general, you will probably have to re-route pipes and cables already in the attic.

Attic conversion work should not be undertaken lightly since major structural alterations to the roof are inevitable. That is why it is essential to employ professionals to carry out at least all the initial design work, loading calculations and the necessary structural alterations. Then, if you want to save money, do the less critical parts of the job yourself: building the dividing partitions, cladding the floor and ceiling, installing the electrical circuits and pipework.

If you do intend carrying out these tasks yourself, and you have any doubts at all regarding your ability to do so, then consult an expert in the particular area. In the final analysis, it may save much frustration, time and cost.

What the job involves

The weight of the floor, partition walls and ceiling of an attic conversion can be quite considerable and that is without the loading imposed by the framework for a dormer and, of course, the furnishings added to the completed rooms. So the very first job that is done when converting the loft is to build a supporting structure that will be able to carry this loading and also provide partial support to the roof, if parts of its original framework have been removed.

1 Installing a new attic floor; after setting the front trimmer across load-bearing walls, checking that it is absolutely level.

2 Laying side trimmers perpendicular to the front trimmer and resting across the original joists; attach them with metal joist hangers.

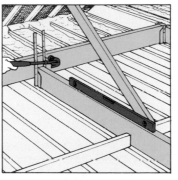

3 Hanging a central cross trimmer between the side trimmers to support a partition wall; pack it out over supporting walls below.

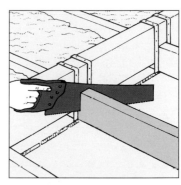

4 After installing a stairwell trimmer between the side trimmers to support the existing joists; cutting through to form the well.

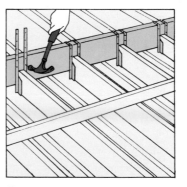

5 Hanging new joists between the side trimmers; lay a straight-edge across the front and central trimmers as a guide to their level.

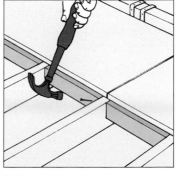

6 Toe-nailing bracing between the joists to support the edges of the plywood flooring panels; stagger the joints between panels.

Strengthening the floor

It is most unlikely that the original attic joists will be capable of providing the necessary extra support. There are two ways in which a strong floor frame can be made: either extra joists of the same size as the originals are fitted between them, or a completely separate structure is built on top of them, being supported directly by the load-bearing walls. Of the two, the latter is preferable, since it will insulate the rooms below from noise and vibration from the rooms above. It will also prevent damage to the ceiling during the construction stage. However, the available headroom will be reduced.

The separate framework will consist of strong wooden beams called trimmers placed around the edges and at strategic points joists will be fitted between them on metal hangers. Where trimmers and joists pass over intermediate loadbearing walls they are packed out with wood blocks for support.

Once this framework is in place, the necessary modifications can be made to the roof itself – adding extra support struts, dormer frameworks and even, in some cases, loadbearing wood-framed partitions.

The floor is normally clad with tongued-and-grooved plywood sheets — a quickly-laid, flat floor.

The stairs

It is possible to buy standard size flights of stairs, either of the closed or open tread type and, if at all possible, these should be chosen to save on the expense of having stairs specially made to fit. It may be necessary to add a trimmer joist to the floor at the foot of the stairs for extra strength; another trimmer will be needed in the attic floor to support the top. The opening for the new stairs will be quite large and roomy, requiring several original attic joists to be cut through. Their ends must be supported from the new framework with trimmer joists or metal hangers.

The staircase itself may need cladding along the underside with gypsumboard, unless it is of the open-tread variety.

The ceiling and walls

Joists for the ceiling can be nailed between the original rafters, and if a dormer is fitted they are bolted in place and carried through to support the dormer roof.

The internal walls can be lightweight stud partitions. The frames should be nailed together flat on the floor and then lifted into position where they can be nailed to the floor joists, the ceiling joists and to the rafters or other parts of the structure. Always notch the frameworks to fit over the existing roof members, not the other way round otherwise you will weaken the roof.

Doorways

Doorways can be made in the usual fashion and a useful tip here is to save the section of sole plate cut from the opening and use it as a lintel above the door.

While the ceiling and partition frameworks are bare, you can fit all the electrical accessory mounting boxes to battens nailed in place and run in all the cables and any pipework. Then cut insulation material to fit between the studs and bracing of the walls, the joists of the ceiling and the original rafters.

Wall cladding

Clad the walls and ceilings with foil-backed gypsumboard. This will help insulate the rooms and prevent moisture from passing through the walls into the roof space. The final job is to plaster the walls (see page 19) and decorate.

You will need to be able to get to the rest of the roof for repairs and maintenance to water tanks and pipework, in addition to using it for storage purposes.

To this end, hatches should be built into the partition frameworks. They can be fitted with plywood panels held by magnetic catches and trimmed with molding.

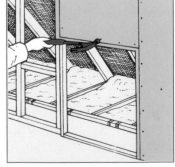

1 Framing the sides of the stairwell with bevel-topped posts nailed to the rafters above and the ends of the joists below.

2 Dividing up the attic space into rooms with intermediate partition walls; these should be leveled and fixed to rafters where possible.

3 Nailing lining timbers around an access hatch after cutting through the framework and inserting a trimmer over the opening.

4 Cladding the partition with foil-backed gypsumboard nailed to the studwork, foil side outwards, and butting up to the lining.

BUILDING AN EXTENSION

A ground floor extension can be purpose-designed and built to suit your needs exactly, or it can be constructed from a number of standard prefabricated components purchased from an extension manufacturer. Which type you choose depends on what you will use it for. The former is ideal for bathrooms, kitchens, bedrooms, living rooms; the latter is more suited to laundry rooms, sun rooms, children's play rooms, work-shops and so on, and includes simple metal-framed, full-glazed conservatories.

The foundations

The most important parts of the structure of your new extension are the foundations, which support the walls and spread the load evenly across the ground. Consequently, their design is quite critical and should be carried out after consulting your local Building Code which will specify the type of foundations required for the job and the depth to which they must be dug, based on local ground conditions.

To be effective, foundations must lie on firm, stable sub-soil, and depending on the soil type this may mean digging to a depth of 3ft or more. The type of soil will also dictate the type of foundations needed, as will the method of construction of the extension.

Types of foundation

For a purpose-built extension with brick or block walls, it is usual to lay concrete in a trench and build the walls on top but for lighter constructions, such as prefabricated buildings, a slab of concrete known as a "raft" is more common.

Strip foundations

The most common form of foundation is the "strip" type. With these a layer of concrete at least 6in thick is spread along the bottom of the trench, leveled off, then the walls built on top. Normally, a width of 18in is quite adequate, but at depths below 3ft or on certain types of weak soil a width of 30in or more is preferable – often with steel reinforcement added.

Trench-fill foundations

The trench-fill foundation is filled with concrete to within 6in of the ground level and the walls begun.

The concrete for this type of foundation should be at least 20in deep and about 6in wider than the width of the wall. The sides of the trench must be vertical to prevent any possibility of the load above causing the foundations to topple.

Constructing the walls

The walls of a habitable extension to your house must be of cavity construction; that is comprising an outer leaf of bricks and an inner leaf of bricks or, more usually, concrete insulating blocks with a 2in air gap in between giving a wall thickness of 11in, although the cavity may be 3in wide to accommodate polystyrene slab insulation and still leave an air gap.

Even if the main part of your house has solid outer walls, the Building Code specifies that your extension must be of cavity wall construction.

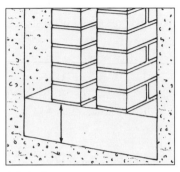

1 Strip foundations require a depth of 6in and a width of 18in on normal subsoil; no reinforcement is needed.

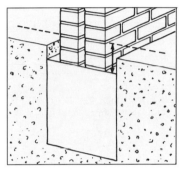

2 Saving time on bricklaying using a trench-fill foundation. Excavate at least 26in deep, and 6in wider than the wall.

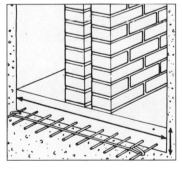

3 On soft subsoils a wide strip foundation is used to spread load; reinforcement used if it projects more than its thickness.

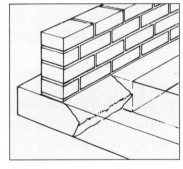

4 To join on to an existing foundation, cut back the joining edge to a V-shape to provide a good key for the new concrete.

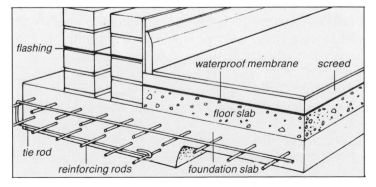

Raft foundations, used when building an extension, need careful design; consult your local Building Inspector or Engineer.

Catering for drain pipes

An important consideration when building an extension is the position of any drainage pipe run – either an existing one from the house or any new waste pipes from fittings in the new extension. You must sort out the route the pipes will take before the walls are built since they will pass through them below floor level, and openings must be left in the walls as they are built. Lintels will need to be incorporated to support the wall above the openings. If the extension is to have trench-fill foundations, ducts should be made in the concrete to allow the passage of pipes. A simple method is to set slightly larger pipes in the concrete as it is poured and then run the pipes through these round openings later.

Positioning a plastic cavity-wall tie sloping down towards the outer leaf. The ribbed ends ensure high pull-out strength, and drip rings prevent water from crossing the cavity; the flexible plastic accommodates uneven courses.

Marking out

The positions of the inner and outer leaves of the walls should be marked centrally on the concrete of the foundations with chalk. The center lines of the wall and foundations being within 1in of each other.

As the walls are built, stringlines are stretched between the corners to make sure each course of bricks or blocks is laid in a straight line.

Cavity wall construction

Although you can use brick for both inner and outer leaves of the wall, in practice it makes more sense to use lightweight concrete blocks for the former since these will provide a certain amount of insulation – a requirement of the Building Regulations.

With this type of construction, the inner leaf is the load-bearing part of the wall, carrying the weight of any floors and ceilings so lintels must be fitted across doorways and windows. Steel boot lintels are best since they are relatively lightweight and their shape ensures that any water that penetrates the outer leaf of the wall is prevented from reaching the inner leaf and is channeled out over the toe of the boot.

The two leaves of the wall should be constructed simultaneously, laying a few courses of each at a time. As construction proceeds, the two leaves must be linked together with metal or plastic wall ties to

1 Laying a batten, with strings attached for later removal, across wall ties to prevent mortar from falling into cavity.

2 Building up inner leaf; lay a bed of mortar along blocks below, butter end of block with mortar and tap into position.

3 Building up outer leaf of brick; build up corners first, stretch a string-line between and fill in middle up to line.

4 Closing cavity at window and door openings; turn inner leaf and insert a vertical DPC between it and outer leaf.

prevent them leaning away from each other. Ties are designed to prevent water running across them to the inner leaf but they must still be set in the mortar joints so that they slope downwards slightly towards the outer leaf. Ties should be set about 18in apart vertically and 3ft apart horizontally, the positions in each horizontal row being staggered with those above and below. At door and window openings, ties should be set one above the other at 12in intervals.

Water penetration must also be prevented from below and this is achieved by inserting a flexible bitumen damp-proof course (DPC) in a horizontal mortar joint around the base of each leaf, at least two courses of bricks above ground level. When the floor is laid, a damp-proof membrane (DPM) is taken up the walls and tucked under the DPC. Strips of DPC must be fitted in the vertical mortar joints where the inner leaf is turned to close off the cavity at windows and door openings, and below the threshold of the door, linking to the DPC in the outer leaf.

The walls must be toothed into the existing house walls at alternate courses to ensure permanent stability (see page 37).

Flat roof construction

The method used for constructing a flat roof is outlined in the following way; the joists usually being laid along the length of the extension from the house to the end wall. At the house end, the joists may either rest on top of a wooden wall plate, being toe-nailed in place, or be nailed to metal hangers which are also nailed to the wall plate. The ends of the wall plate are set in sockets built into the extension side walls.

At the end of the extension, the joists can simply rest on top of the end wall and be nailed in place or, if there is a window in the end wall, a second wooden beam can be fitted to span the opening and support the joists.

Tapered furring pieces are nailed to the tops of the joists to create the right fall. For felt covering the fall should be 1 in 60, but for asphalt it should be 1 in 80.

Sheets of exterior grade plywood are used to provide a roof decking and are nailed down through the furring pieces into the joists. The sheets should be staggered so the joints between their short edges do not coincide.

Covering with asphalt

Although a felt-covered roof is the cheapest and easiest to construct, a much more durable finish can be obtained by having it covered with asphalt. This material is heated until it melts and is then spread over the roof to provide a solid, impervious layer when it cools. It is a job that requires a great deal of skill and is one that you should get a building contractor to do for you.

Flat roofs can often suffer from condensation when moist air passes through the ceiling from the rooms below and cools on contact with the underside of the roof — particularly with bathrooms and kitchens and when the atmosphere is damp.

Leaving ventilation gaps behind the fascia and insulating the roof will help, but the best idea is to either use foil-back gypsumboard for the ceiling – which will stop the moist air passing through – or staple a separate polyethelene vapor barrier to the underside of the joists before nailing the gypsumboard in place. Once the extension has been weatherproofed by glazing the windows and fitting the doors, the room can be finished. Before plastering the walls and ceiling, lay in the necessary electrical cables, mount accessory boxes and run in any pipework for hot and cold water or central heating.

1 Nailing the roof joists into hangers attached to the main beam; toe-nail through the top of the roof joists into the main beam also.

2 Nailing furring pieces (narrow end over the front wall) to the tops of the roof joists to set a 1 in 80 fall for the roof covering.

3 Nailing the plywood roofing sheets over the furrings; stagger the joints between the short edges.

4 After pouring hot asphalt onto the roof, smoothing it out to a layer about ⅜in thick.

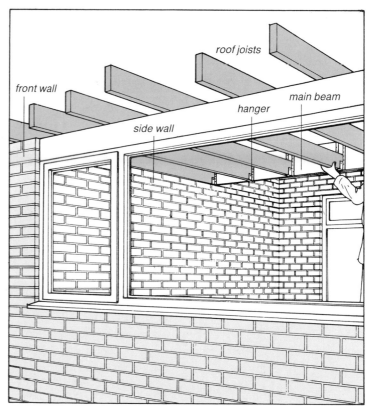

Resting the roof joists between the front wall and the main beam which has been set into the side walls of the extension.

INDEX